Compiled and Edited by Jim Reese

Recollections of
Thad Morgan
The Man Who Could Make
God Cuss...And Laugh

outskirts
press

Table of Contents

Teachers and Other Employees

Central Office / System Administrators

Superintendents, Principals, and Other Administrators

Coaches

Who Was Thad Morgan?

Facebook Posts Following Thad Morgan's Death

Selected Passages from Perry Vickers' Eulogy at Thad Morgan's Funeral

Final Personal Thoughts

Introduction

It was late May 1975. It was Graduation Night for those students who were receiving their Enterprise High School diplomas at Bates Memorial Stadium in Enterprise, Alabama. The stadium had been completed in 1956 and it had become a tradition for graduations to be held there.

Thad Morgan was completing his first year as Principal at Enterprise High School. He had served as one of the assistant principals at the school prior to his becoming principal so he knew practically all of the seniors who were to graduate. He had already gotten a reputation as a strict disciplinarian who was not afraid to use corporal punishment. In fact he used a paddle quite often. He especially liked to demonstrate his expertise with that wooden instrument on the rear ends of football players.

It had also become a custom for those graduating to walk across a platform on the football field as their names were called and to be congratulated with a handshake by the principal of the school. The grads received fake diplomas on the platform and following the ceremony would go to the high school building and get their real diplomas from their homeroom teachers.

On this particular night Roger, the first name of a huge offensive lineman who was a terrific player on our outstanding football team, had his name called. After Roger took his "diploma," he shook Mr. Morgan's hand. However, he did more than shake his hand. He squeezed it so hard that Mr. Morgan said that he thought his hand was broken. That did not keep Roger from uttering the following words, "YOU WON'T WHIP MY ASS ANYMORE, FAT BOY!!"

Mr. Morgan did not want to make a scene at that time. Instead, following the ceremony, he sprinted to the high school, found Roger's homeroom teacher, and got Roger's real diploma. A few minutes later, Roger went to Mr. Morgan's office and notified Mr. Morgan that his homeroom teacher did not have his diploma. Mr. Morgan pointed to his desk with a paddle on top of a document. He then told Roger, "It is right here, Sugar Boy, and you're going to get one more ass beating before you get it!!" Sure enough, Roger got one more ass beating.

(Ed.'s note) Mr. Morgan and I laughed about this story many times before he passed away. I also confirmed the story with Roger in a telephone conversation a couple of weeks before I finished the manuscript. Roger laughed about the incident as well.

If you continue reading this book, you will find many other stories about Thad Morgan that will make you laugh, cry, cringe, and perhaps say "That could not have happened." I assure you what the contributors to this book reported did happen.

I suppose it was 1972-73 during my second year of teaching at Enterprise High School that Thad became a second father to me. I was teaching psychology, sociology, and world history that year. One day during the final period of the day during a psychology class a male student continued to talk after I had told him to stop. When he refused, I told him quite loudly to "SHUT THE HELL UP!"

Early the next morning before the students arrived, Thad entered my classroom and talked with me about the improper language I had used the day before. I thought to myself, "Well isn't this the pot calling the kettle black?" I was well aware of Thad's propensity for cursing. However, his words made more sense to me when he told me that the boy to whom I had used the foul language was the son of a school board member. I was lucky Thad talked with me calmly rather than giving me a loud "butt chewing" that he was famous for.

Thad served as Principal of EHS from 1974-1979. He then was named Superintendent of Education and served in that position from 1979-2001. With the exception of one year, I worked with Thad in the Central Office from July 1, 1985 until he retired. I succeeded him and served as Superintendent from July 1, 2001 through December 31, 2010. I suppose it was like Ray Perkins succeeding Bear Bryant. I knew I was no Thad Morgan, but I had enough common sense not to try to be him.

Thad would be upset with me if I did not "sing the praises" of Gladys Welch, the Secretary for both of us and who was our "right arm." Godzilla, as Thad called her, kept us both in line and could do more work in the shortest amount of time than anyone I have ever known. She passed away approximately three months after Thad's death. I regret her health would not allow her to contribute some stories to this book before she died.

Having read all the entries to this book, I hope that you will see the respect and admiration that so many people had for Thad Morgan – a man whose positive influence will permeate not only our generation but many future generations.

This book is certainly not an exhaustive compilation of stories about Thad but can be considered a highlight reel of each stage of his life.

Acknowledgments

I would like to thank many people for making this book possible. First, I am grateful that Janice and Bill Morgan put their confidence in me to attempt such a project as this one. This book is certainly better than anything I could have done as a sole biographer.

Next, I sincerely appreciate everyone who contributed their recollections of Thad Morgan. Your memories and stories brought me laughter at times, tears at times and always enjoyment. I am well aware that there are many people who will ask me, "Why didn't you ask me to share my memories and/or stories of Thad?" I apologize for not contacting you and will blame it on my feeble mind. An even bigger apology goes to anyone who submitted an entry to the book that was inadvertently omitted.

One individual who provided much help in various ways was Pam McQueen. I have known Pam and her family for a long time, and I have never seen her seek personal recognition for anything she has accomplished or done.

Another person who came through immediately before I completed the manuscript was Caroline Quattlebaum who found some pictures from the files of the newspaper *The Southeast Sun*. Some of them are also included in the book. Caroline, her father Howard Quattlebaum and brother Russell operated that newspaper for many years. As an aside, Howard was the radio voice along with color commentator Harrell Thompson for the Enterprise Wildcat football team for several years.

Many of my family members became engaged in this endeavor. My wife Marcy, my sister Rhonda Reese Parker, my daughter Tiffany Dowling, and my son Brad Reese gave me not only moral support but also shared their ideas and knowledge of technology as we went through the process of developing the book. Hayley O'Neal was a tremendous help in preparing the manuscript.

Finally, I want to thank Tina Ruvalcaba, Elaine Simpson and their colleagues at Outskirts Press for their competency, courtesy, and patience in seeing that this book got published.

**Only God Can
Make A Thad
&
Only Thad Can
Make God Cuss**

A Message From God

One stormy day in March
When things were going bad
The Lord looked down upon the earth
And said "It's time to create Thad."

To create such a creature
Will really be a test,
This man will have his own strange style,
Different from the rest.

His life will not be easy
For the jobs that he must do,
But when the tough days come around,
I will see him through.

I'll start at the beginning
With the most important part
Though he may try to hide it,
He'll need a caring heart.

His brain – a little different,
He'll do things that cause some fright.
But he knows what he is doing,
And he's doing what is right.

Now we get down to the parts
Where I won't take the blame
They help to make him who he is
They go along with his name.

He will growl like a pit bull,
He will rant and rave and rumble,
He'll shake his finger in your face
And he'll walk away and mumble.

He'll chew on his tobacco
Looking for a place to spit.
Never bring him a petition
Or he'll have a holy fit.

He'll cuss and fuss and say some things
That really cause me woe.
He will quickly speak his mind
And his favorite word is No.

He will not flinch an inch
As he paddles grown-up men
For something they did yesterday
Or some long forgotten sin.
I can see he'll need some help
To steer him through the troubled times.
I'll create a quiet and gentle saint
And call her Janice Grimes.

I'll start him out as a football coach
To learn the rules of life,
So he can be a leader
Who won't quit when there is strife.

There may be one small problem
As he ends his coaching days,
I foresee him pacing the sidelines
And trying to call the plays.

Thad will need some training
From a man with a strong voice
Who is a pro at running schools
And I think I'll call him Royce.

Thad must learn to manage money,
Students, staff, and parents too,
When it comes to Enterprise Schools
Second best won't do.

When he interviews and hires personnel
He will always go first class
He won't tolerate excuses
Or a job that's done half-ass.

Power, control, authority
Can sometimes be abused
I'll need someone with guts of steel
To see that it's wisely used.

If Thad starts getting out of line
It will be her job to squelch.
I'll create a strong tough lady
God bless you, Gladys Welch.

It's time to add the good traits
And the good out-weigh the bad.
Respect, responsibility
This too is part of Thad.

Tenacity, trust, commitment
Appointed school boards, discipline, pride
These things you can depend on
Their roots run deep inside.
He will not like a show.
He'll do more good in quiet ways
Than you will ever know.

For the students in this city
He'll put up one hell of a fight.
He'll support his staff 100%
If what they are doing is right.

I will give him a sense of humor
Somewhat warped, but it will do.
If you get down and need a friend
He'll come shining through.

The plans are made; it's time to work.
It's getting very late.
But before I begin this challenge
Let's set the record straight.

I will make the world a promise.
Please don't panic; please don't run.
When I create Thad Morgan.
I'm only making one.

This poem was written by Mary Cannon for Thad Morgan on Bosses Day October 16, 1996. It was read by Kevin Maddox during his tribute to Coach Morgan at the funeral service for him at the EHS Performing Arts Center on March 15, 2023.

Janice Morgan

From a Conversation with Jim Reese 2023

Before Thad Morgan's birth his parents were told by the doctor that Mrs. Morgan was not pregnant but instead had a "fibroid tumor." This was still their belief until a short time before Thad was born. Thad's wife Janice said that after they were married, anytime she wanted to make him angry she would remind him that he was only a "fibroid tumor."

When Thad announced to his parents that he and Janice were getting married, his mother "hit the panic button." Janice learned that after she and Thad had left from announcing their plans, Thad's mother asked Thad's father, "Ed, what if Janice's parents won't send her to college if she marries?"

Ed's response was, "Well, I've always wanted a little girl; I guess WE can send her." Mrs. Morgan was unaware that Janice was graduating from college that year. Thad's mother was greatly relieved to learn that.

After graduating from college, Janice got a teaching job at Geneva, a small town near Enterprise. Herbert Hawkins, Thad's former Head Football Coach at Enterprise High School, had become the Principal of Geneva High School. Janice taught English that year and indicated that she had a very good one. The other English teacher in her grade did not give her a vote of confidence because she thought the students would "run over" her but soon she was seeing that Janice had good classroom management.

Thad was happy that Janice was going to work for Coach Hawkins. Thad had much respect for him. Coach Hawkins always checked his football players' report cards after each grading period, and Thad did the same thing when he became a coach. Thad saw Coach Hawkins' discipline in a personal way when Thad played for Coach Hawkins. On a Friday afternoon before an out of town game when Thad was in high school, he got a barber to give him a "Mohawk" haircut. When Thad arrived at the school to dress for the game, Coach Hawkins saw the new hair style and was not amused. He made Thad put on his football helmet and not remove it until the team arrived back home from the game.

Thad's mentor was Royce Snellgrove. Mr. Snellgrove served as Superintendent of Education of the Enterprise City Schools from 1953-1972 (in 1953 the secondary schools that were part of the county school system became part of the Enterprise system). When Thad started work in the Enterprise City School System in 1967 until Mr. Snellgrove retired, Thad got "fired" 10 times by his mentor. They would often get into some heated discussions. Thad's Secretary Gladys Welch always told Thad to "Calm down – he'll be back."

As predicted, Mr. Snellgrove would come back in the afternoon and tell Thad, "Let's go get a Coke."

Thad and Janice Morgan

*Standing L-R Janice,
Cornelia (Bitsy), Bill,
and Thad Morgan
Seated Janice's Parents
Mr. and Mrs. Grimes*

Thad's Path after High School

Written By Mike and Pam McQueen

After graduating from Enterprise High School in 1956, Thad attended and played football for Marion Institute for the 1956 and 1957 seasons. He then attended and played football for the Troy State Trojans "Red Waves" for the 1958 and 1959 seasons. On August 13, 1959 he married Janice Grimes, daughter of Mr. and Mrs. Fred Grimes at her parents' home in Coffee Springs, Alabama. After finishing at Troy, the young couple moved to Marietta, Georgia where Thad accepted a job as the football coach at R.L. Osborne Junior High School and was also an assistant at Osborne High School for the 1960 football season.

At the time the head coach at R.L. Osborne High School was Milford Young. Thad coached there for two years before accepting the head coaching position at Villa Rica High School in Georgia. In August of 1963 when Milford Young became the head coach at Warner Robins High School, Thad was hired to be the line coach there.

After Thad's parents were brutally murdered at their home on June 22, 1964, Thad resigned his position at Warner Robins High School in July of that same year and returned to Enterprise to "manage family property." He was hired by the Geneva County School System in the fall of 1964 to be a teacher/assistant coach at Coffee Springs. Thad served as the Head Football Coach at Coffee Springs for the 1965-66 seasons.

Thad resigned at the end of the first semester of the 1966-67 school year and accepted the Head Football Coach position at Enterprise Junior High School beginning the second semester of that year. He served in that position for the 1967, 1968, and 1969 seasons where he compiled a record of 18-2 with the only two losses coming in his first year. He was also the Head Basketball Coach at EJHS and had an outstanding record in that position as well.

In 1970 Thad joined the Enterprise High School coaching staff as an assistant under Paul Terry. In 1972 he was still an assistant coach at EHS and also became an assistant principal under Charles Howell. Before the school system fully integrated in 1970, Alfred Peavy was a coach at Coppinville High School. He became an Assistant Principal at EHS in 1971 and served in that position for many years. Howell, Thad and Peavy were instrumental in the smooth transition of integration of EHS in the early 1970s. Thad was named Principal of Enterprise High School when Mr. Howell became an assistant to Superintendent Jack Rutland who had replaced Royce Snellgrove in 1972. Thad was named Superintendent of Education of the Enterprise City School in 1979 and remained in that position or 22 years.

L-R: Thad Morgan, Charles Howell, and Alfred Peavy

The Early Years

Bo Lee

EHS Class of 1956

Cactus Cal

If you grew up in the Wiregrass in the early days of home television, you remember well small-screen black and white TV shows. If you were a cowboy show fan as so many of us were, you also remember many thirty-minute episodes that contained a complete adventure full of shoot-'em-ups and damsels in distress. If your home had a really good antenna, you could pick up two stations, one in Montgomery and one in Dothan, and be selective about what you watched. Many a young lad though loved to watch Cactus Cal, the best of *The Cactus Cal Show*, who introduced each day's cowboy thriller on WSFA-TV. Dressed in his full cowboy regalia, he invited the youngsters in his audience to write him and send a photo, both of which he would share at the end of the program.

One day Cactus Cal showed a letter and photo from an avid fan in Enterprise. The young man told ol' Cactus Cal how he looked forward to the show every afternoon. In fact, he loved that show so much he hurried home from football practice at the high school so that he would not miss a minute of each day's show. Cactus finished reading the fan letter and held up a photo of none other than Thad Morgan.

Everyone began calling Thad Cactus Cal after the news spread about his letter, and he was "Cactus Cal" until he graduated from Enterprise High School.

But I knew that someone else had to have written that letter and played a big trick on Bad Thad. You see, every day when we finished football practice – and even after games – Thad was the absolute last player out of the locker room.

I would get out to the parking lot and see Mrs. Morgan sitting in their Frazer waiting for her son. Many a time she called me over to her window to ask if Thad was still in the locker room, and I would have to answer "Yes, every time."

Finally, she asked me why he was always the last one out of the locker room. I had to tell the truth.

"Mrs. Morgan," I answered, "Thad is just really slow."

That's how I knew he didn't write that fan letter. He was never home in time to watch the show, but we never did know who did send it. So, here's to you, Cactus Cal!

Ed. Note – Ann Lammon Day confessed that she and Jacqueline Thompson were the practical jokers.

CULVERTS, POLITICS, AND A SENIOR SUMMER

I met Thad fairly soon after I moved to Enterprise in 1946. He was in school and in church with me. I learned quickly that in either place he was likely to provoke a fight if he could. Why? I guess because he just liked to fight. In fact, that tendency is how he got his nickname Bad Thad.

Bad Thad might be attending Royal Ambassadors at First

Baptist Church as all good boys did, but what he was really doing was scouting out the next person he might fight. Then after we fellows in RAs were released but while still on the church grounds, Thad and the selected sparring partner would slug it out. This scenario was repeated endlessly at church and school. Charles Rowe, who lived behind the church, and Edward Justice, son of the Baptist preacher, were his best friends. In fact, everyone liked Thad, in spite of his proclivity for picking fights.

Perhaps his pugnacious behavior, though, was why John Knowles, later a lawyer in Geneva but at the time a fellow football player in Enterprise, *intentionally* knocked out Thad's front teeth. On the football practice field! When Bad Thad was in the 9th grade! And John was a junior with playing experience!

Thad's mother Estelle was somehow related to Big Jim Folsom, former governor of Alabama. She also worked at the courthouse in Enterprise for years. I think her connections might be why Thad and I and another friend got jobs working for the State of Alabama the summer after we graduated from EHS. The rest of the summer crew was from Elba. The way they singled us out, they probably thought we didn't deserve the jobs.

All 10 of us were labeled "surveying crew," but we spent a great deal of time just riding around in the Carry-All. Any work that actually got done was quite frequently done by Thad and me while the others continued to ride around in the Carry-All. (Well, all 10 of us did manage to measure, mark, and paint the well-traveled Highway 231from Ozark to Ariton using a 100-foot tape measure, nails and bottle caps, and paint brushes and hammers and without using any protective gear whatsoever.)

One day we were loaded into the Carry-All and taken to Clayhatchee, where Thad and I were told to get out. We were left there to work without being told what work we were to accomplish. Later in the day, the Carry-All returned, picked us up, and finally stopped at the underpass leading into downtown Enterprise. Thad and I were told to disembark.

The crew boss led us to the opening into a large pipe near the railroad track. He told us to go into the pipe, follow it to the end, and measure the distance from one end to the other. We looked at the dark, dirty pipe, looked at one another, and together asked, "Why us?" The boss winked and said, "I don't trust the others to do it." The fellows left in the truck were laughing and hooting and gesturing at us as Thad and I entered the pipe.

Imagine a pipe tall enough for grown boys to be able to almost stand up in. Imagine a pipe that had been there for decades and never been cleaned. Imagine a pipe many animals had made their home.

Imagine what those animals had done in that pipe.

Imagine the pipe growing smaller and smaller in diameter the further we walked, crawled, and slithered into it.

Imagine a pipe long enough to go underground, past the current police station and city hall.

Imagine how mad Bad Thad was getting the further we inched into the pipe. Imagine what Thad threatened to do to the rest of the crew as soon as we got out of said pipe.

When we got out, however, the Carry-All had disappeared with all the crew in it. I do not remember ever reporting the length of the pipe to anyone.

Being Thad's friend over many decades has always been a pleasure, but that one time I think I was the victim of being his friend. And I was just relieved that he didn't want to fight me – for lack of having anyone better on hand – once we staggered back into the fading sunlight.

Bless Thad's heart. He gave the rest of his life working to make his community a better place.

Thad Morgan – Enterprise Wildcat!

Jack Lindsey

Classmate of Thad From Grades 1-12

I first met Thad Morgan in the first grade. I had to go the bathroom. That is where I met Thad. He had a friend whose name was Charles Rowe. Charles was short, muscular and tough and was also in the bathroom. Thad guarded the bathroom door because he and Charles did not have permission to be in there. That was the beginning of our friendship that lasted the rest of our lives.

When Thad was in the 10th grade, he was a very determined young man who would just not give up. I saw him get two teeth knocked out during football practice one day, and he kept on practicing. He was like this his entire life. That same year Humphrey Bogart was a movie star who played mostly tough man roles. Some of the girls we hung around with got to saying Thad looked like the actor so Thad earned the nickname Bogart the rest of our years in high school.

One summer Thad decided he would go to Panama City Beach to get a job. My girl friend took him to the Bellwood Highway that was the best spot to hitchhike for a ride. After eventually catching a ride, Thad arrived at the beach and landed a job working on a garbage truck. That job lasted 4-5 weeks before he returned home.

Thad was the worst driver I have ever seen. He and I were in Geneva one night seeing some friends. I had a small 1948 Chevy Coupe, and I let Thad drive. We went to the junction where the Choctawhatchee and Pea Rivers meet. The water was high on both sides. As Thad was driving my vehicle, he backed it up to within 15 feet of the river with all of us still in the car. He seemed unconcerned.

One weekend Thad, Billy Dean Powers, Jack Powers, and I went to Panama City Beach. On Saturday night after a few hours at "The Hangout," we looked for a place to sleep. Back then there were not places late at night on the beach. We stopped at a little drive-in restaurant similar to the Hob Nob in Enterprise. Thad just had to have a hamburger at 2:30 in the morning. Before we went in, Thad had to relieve himself so he walked around to the back of the place. Suddenly, he heard this man pleading, "Let me sleep." Thad knew the guy was a "street person" and made him get up from sleeping and eat a burger with us at 3:00 A.M. I will never forget that poor man.

When our middle son Chris got to high school, Thad was Superintendent of Education. Chris would come home and tell me Mr. Morgan would walk up and lightly kick him in the rear. I know that was Thad's way of saying, "I like you."

I always looked at our children's report cards. One day one of our sons came home, and I asked to see his report card. He handed it to me slowly. After I looked at his card, I noticed a small correction on one subject. Boy, had our soon been caught! I loaded him in the car and headed to the high school.

I had an open door policy with Thad so I just walked into his office and told him what my son had done hoping that Thad would "jump on hm." Thad laughed and told my son to be in his office the next morning. When my son came home that afternoon, I asked him what Thad did. He told me that Mr. Morgan said, "Boy, you hurt your dad's heart." That's all he said and did. What a great correction for my son!

Ann Lammon Day

As a child, my best friend and playmate was Linda Lou Carmichael. She lived across the street from Charles Rowe who was best friend to Thad Morgan. During the summers I spent a lot of time visiting Linda, and many times Charles and Thad would come over and we would play together. I remember that we had cap guns and wore a belt with a "scabbard" to hold our guns when we were not engaged in battle firing off a roll of caps!

We were all cowboys. I don't remember anyone being an Indian. We got to be real close friends as summers went by. We would sit around and tell scary stories and tell what we thought were dirty jokes! We spent a lot of time just talking. I remember one conversation when they both were emphatic saying when they married that they did not want their wives to work. I think that was their way for a nine-year old to flirt. They were two grades ahead of me, and they were good friends with my brother Elmer Lammon so I saw them often.

When we were teens, we all went to Panama City Beach to the "Hangout" and to "bop!" All of us girls (Phyllis Thomason, Linda Ellis, Sandra Mixson, Martha Jane Rhodes, others and me) had learned to do the PC Bop by practicing with a door knob for a partner. Phyllis and Linda were two of the best from the entire state. We danced with guys from all over. Not very many guys from Enterprise could bop but would watch.

I remember one AEA (Spring Break) THAD ROUGH HOUSE MORGAN and two of his friends, COW JORDAN (Bobby) and PEA RIVER TRAWICK (Donnie), all three football players at EHS, were watching and Thad motioned me over and said, "Ann, if anybody messes with y'all, just let us know." Always the tough guy!

Later when Thad was a junior at Troy State, I began my freshman year there. I don't remember why, but Troy held a girls track meet and of course I volunteered to participate. I fell flat on my face and knocked a front tooth out. I carried on as though I was in extreme pain (I had false teeth but didn't want anyone to know). Thad appeared out of nowhere and told me that he would take me home to my dentist, and he did. Later when he would tell that story, and he told it often, he would say that he was drunk as hell but that I didn't know it. He wasn't. Another ROUGH HOUSE attempt to hide the fact that he was empathetic, caring, kind and loving.

As the years went by, I eventually earned my degree from Auburn at age 40 and returned to Enterprise seeking a job at EHS as a Marketing Education teacher so guess who interviewed me, recommended me for the job and was my boss! Yes, my old friend was now Superintendent of Education Thad. He was my good friend the rest of his life.

Herb Gannon

EHS Class of 1964

I am honored to be asked to comment on my friendship with That Morgan but already know I will be unable to do him or my love for him justice.

Except for remembering my hatred of going to kindergarten at age 5, the first memories of my life include Thad. About the time I was first allowed to go to the "City Pool" off E. Lee St. and not take swimming lessons was when I was about 6 or 7. Usually I was accompanied by brother, Frank, and/or a couple of other friends to splash around on the shallow side of "the rope."

"No hanging on the rope or running" was the most frequent daily command of whoever the lifeguards were in those days of the fifties. But one day this older guy came up, grabbed me, and tossed me into the air. When I came up for air, he grabbed and tossed me again. It was Thad. He must have been 14 or 15 then as I later knew he was about 8 years older than I. Why he picked me out to toss that day I've never known, but it began an indescribable friendship that lasted until his death.

As I passed through Jr. High and EHS, he was by then in other towns progressing in his career. So, in my major formative years, Thad was not present. Had he been, besides my father, he would have been one of the few men responsible for molding me into what I hope was a credible young man (A salute to Coaches Terry and Higginbotham). Once we reunited in the mid-seventies, our relationship/friendship continued strongly as one of deep love and respect for each other.

We enjoyed a fellowship of seriousness, yet mixed with laugh out loud humor and trash talk. I also often gave him unsolicited advice on how to deal with Jimbo Reese and Mary Cannon which he should have listened to. He never 'went the other way' when he saw me coming, and during our times together, he never failed to ask about my folks. Our partings were always preceded by a firm handshake and a hug.

I must share a story I recently heard from my brother Tim. Thad was Principal at EHS, and one day when Tim was a senior, Thad called him to his office. He said, "I just realized you are about to graduate, and I've never paddled you. Bend over the desk." After two licks, Thad said, "You're a good kid; you can go now." Tim really didn't see the humor in that as I did, but he never got tossed into the pool either.

Finally, one of the distinct honors of my life was Thad allowing his precious wife to come to see me as a patient. I was always supremely honored by any patient I saw, but only one had Thad's approval.

I've tried to come up with a closing description of him, but my vocabulary and emotions have not let me. Yeah, he was an Enterprise icon. He had the Heart of a Champion. But even those descriptions are not good enough. One phrase I hear all along after a death is, "He was a good man," and that's all I need to know about someone. People understand that. Thad Morgan was a good man.

Steve Shiver

I remember one particular football practice at Coffee Springs in the 60s where things were not going well as Coach Morgan wanted it to, and he let us know that in no certain terms. His voice got louder and louder and his face got redder and redder as he was communicating his feelings toward us. At the height of his frustration he accidentally swallowed a large cheek full of chewing tobacco. He never acknowledged it, and I think he tried to hide it, but it was obvious what had happened. We all thought it was funny and wanted to laugh but we knew better. In fact I don't think anyone cracked a smile even though it was hard not to. If my memory is correct, Coach Morgan cut practice a little short that day for probably the first time ever. He didn't appear to be feeling very well.

The halls of Coffee Springs High School were not always the safest place to walk when Coach Morgan was roaming the halls. In fact, if you saw him coming from a distance, you tried to turn and go in the opposite direction. Here is an example why: Coach Morgan usually had his paddle with him, and I turned the corner one day and met him. He called out my last name and asked me if I had done anything that day to deserve a lick. I said, "No sir, Coach, not a thing." He grinned and looked at me and said, "Well today is still early. I'm sure you'll do something later today to deserve it so just come over here and let's get it over with." He told me to bend over and he gave me a pretty hard lick with his paddle. He then started walking away, laughing as he went. That's why you tried to avoid him in the hallway if at all possible.

Mike Wilkes

Thad began teaching and coaching at Coffee Springs High School in the fall of 1964. Tommy Johnson who was the Principal at the school from 1962-1965, recommended Thad for the job. Thad served as the Assistant Football and B-Team Basketball Coach during the 1964-65 school year and Head Football Coach and B-team Basketball Coach from the fall of 1965 through the first semester of 1966. He accepted a position at Enterprise Jr. High School that began the second semester of the 1966-67 school year and taught there through the 1967-70 school year.

Thad was a strict disciplinarian, but the players loved him. He believed in his players being in shape, and we did a lot of running. Ironically, he chewed on a cigar throughout the games. In his 3rd period physical education class he had 15 boys. On some days he would make them crawl around the gym – he called those students his "CCP 1 Boys" – crawl one, cry one, and puke one. He also taught them how to slow dance and how to do the Swing.

One time the principal asked Thad to take two boys who had been suspended home to their parents. On the way to their homes one of the boys said, "Coach Morgan, you do realize there ain't but one of you and there are two of us? "

Thad slammed on brakes and almost put the car on its nose. He told both of boys to "GET OUT!" Both of them started shaking, remained in the car, and eventually made it home.

One of Thad's duties was to drag the baseball field. He used his 1960 Ford and attached a wooden block to the back of his vehicle to smooth the field. One day a boy was driving the car and got it hung on the pitcher's mound. Thad stopped using his car and made the boys pull the wooden block instead. If they were not doing it fast enough, he would take a shaved baseball bat and give them licks.

After some football games, Coach Morgan would have what was called "Bloody Saturdays." Those were Saturdays when practices were held because Coach Morgan didn't think they played hard enough in the previous game (games were usually played on Thursdays). Thad told the team "If you ain't gonna dance every dance, don't dance at all for me."

The 1966 team dressed out only 13 boys, but the team had a winning record. Thad called that team the Iron Men. Although Coach Morgan did not coach the 1967 team because of his accepting the job in Enterprise, the Coffee Springs team won 7 games and lost only one. The players gave a lot of credit for the success to Thad's coaching and mentoring before he left.

Before Coach Morgan passed away, the 1966 football team and cheerleaders had an event that honored him in appreciation for all he had done for them. Thad was presented with a plaque that had engraved "GOAT – GREATEST OF ALL TIME."

Tommy Johnson

I taught and coached at Geneva High School with Thad's wife Janice while Thad finished his senior year at Troy on a football scholarship. They went to Georgia to teach and coach. Thad was in the Masters Degree Program at Auburn when his parents were brutally murdered by an escaped convict from camp Enterprise. He resigned his job in Georgia and came home to Enterprise to deal with his parents' deaths. No job was available through the summer. I was Principal at Coffee Springs School, and I hired him to be an assistant coach where he handled the football program. From this position he dealt with the trial of his parents' murderer.

Thad did an excellent job of coaching at Coffee Springs and was employed by Enterprise Junior High as a coach and P.E. teacher and was later moved to an assistant football coach at Enterprise High School. He was later made an assistant principal at the same time with Coach Alfred Peavy and the two becoming disciplinarians. He later became Principal of Enterprise High. His last move was to become the Enterprise City Schools Superintendent where he remained until retirement.

Ed.'s Note: In 1965 Tommy Johnson was named Dean of Students at Enterprise State Junior College – the first year the institution opened.

Ricky Adams

The late Herman Howell played center for Thad at Coffee Springs High School in the era when the Golden Bears played many of their games on Thursday nights.

During one game, the defender who lined up across the line of scrimmage from Herman would snort and kick at the ground from time to time to aggravate Herman "The German."

At halftime, Thad told Herman, "The next time he does that, I want you to knock the hell out of him!"

Early in the third quarter, the player began his annoying taunting so Herman rose from his center position, stepped across the line of scrimmage and knocked the hell out of the guy, then looked at Thad and hollered, "I got him Coach, I got him!"

Thad responded, "During the play, Herman, during the play!"

Herman drew a penalty for obeying his coach: legend has it, referee Tye Adams penalized the Golden Bears for being offside.

More than once, Thad would have only 11-12 players dress out for games, and the first time it happened, a player asked Coach Morgan, "What happens if one of us gets hurt?"

Thad explained no player had his permission to get hurt.

A key player was sick one week and hadn't practiced a time so after Wednesday's practice Thad went to his house to check on him.

The boy's mother greeted him at the door.

"Yes'm, I just wanted to stop by and see how Johnny's doing," Thad said.

"Well, we sure do appreciate you doin' that. He's some better, but nowhere near well. Would you like to see him?"

"Yes'm, if he's not asleep."

"I believe he's awake. Can I git you a glass of tea?"

"Yes'm, that'd be good."

"Just go in his room, and I'll bring you the tea in there."

While Mama was pouring the tea, Thad went into Johnny's room, snatched him up by his pajama top and said, "You better git your ass out of that bed and be in school and dressed out tomorrow. Hear me, say?"

"Yessir!"

Mama delivered the tea and after Thad drained the glass he said, "I sure appreciate you letting me see Johnny. I feel he's getting better."

"Johnny, now you get a good night's sleep and maybe you'll

feel like going to school tomorrow."

"Yessir, Coach Morgan. I'll try to be there."

"We sure do thank you for comin' by and checkin' on him," Mama said.

Johnny was at school the next day and played the game that night.

Thad took all 12 Golden Bears to Daleville for a September 17, 1965 game and when they arrived, Daleville's Coach Fred Johnson asked Thad where the rest of the team was.

"This is the whole team," Thad, in his first year at CSHS, explained.

After the game Coffee Springs won, 33-6, Johnson, accused Thad of running up the score on the Warhawks, the first football team Daleville fielded.

"Coach, we played everybody on our team," Thad explained. "You had 30 players and we had 12. There wasn't anything I could do."

On Thursday, October 6, 1966, Coffee Springs played at Louisville and when the Bears arrived, the bus driver rolled to a stop near the water tower.

Thad stepped out of the bus and was greeted by Lavon Kelly.

"Where's the field?" Thad asked.

"You're standing on it."

One of the water towers was in the end zone.

Louisville won 34-6.

In the late '70s , when Sherman Wilkinson played football at Troy State University, Thad, Billy Hildreth, Harrell Thompson and I would meet at Thad's office about 4 p.m. home game Saturdays, hop into Harrell's van and head to

Troy, usually with Billy driving, Thad navigating, and Harrell and me In the back seat.

One Saturday, all the way to the stadium, Billy and Thad discussed landing procedures they'd performed during their recent flying lessons. We heard about crosswind landings, three-point landings and possibly even power-off landings they'd made at Crestview, Defuniak Springs, Opp, etc.

Harrell and I were included out of those discussions.

That Saturday, temperatures had dropped dramatically during Troy's win and before we'd gotten very far on our return to Enterprise, the van's windshield began fogging up.

Seriously fogging!

Billy, after fumbling for the defrost switch for what seemed to be an eternity, asked Thad to help find it...which he did...help find it.

To no avail.

Finally, one of 'em asked Harrell how to turn on the defroster;

Harrell quickly instructed 'the crew' and the switch was imme-diately activated.

Once we could see the road, Harrell asked, "Adams, would you get off the ground in any kind of airplane if either one of those two fools in the front seat, who can't even turn on the defroster in a van, was the pilot?"

Charles Platt

First impressions can sometimes be deceiving. After six years at city school later known as College Street Elementary, a select group of young boys and girls moved up to "Old Junior High" right down the street. It was in the seventh grade at "Old Junior" that we learned about physical education with our instructor Mr. Morgan. Our first look at Mr. Morgan was a large man with a crew cut driving a 1964 Chevrolet Biscayne white or cream in color with a beautiful striping from Mr. Morgan's favorite chew of tobacco.

Mr. Morgan would arrive at the first bell each morning in front of the old gymnasium where he would slide in the gravel pit by throwing the vehicle into park before it actually stopped. It was in physical education that we learned the meaning of short and long laps around the campus. We also learned the swing style of Mr. Morgan's paddle if we left any of our clothing on the floor in the dressing room after physical education. He was bigger than life and tougher than nails to a bunch of six graders now graduated into the seventh grade.

It was a surprise to us when Mr. Morgan graduated eighth grade with us and moved on to Enterprise High School where he was a teacher, coach and later Assistant Principal. Many interesting stories have been told and will continue to be told about Mr. Morgan and his days at Enterprise High School. Tough as nails, yes, but it's later in life that one realizes that the man had a heart bigger than the old Bates Memorial Stadium.

On several occasions Mr. Morgan was under treatment for different types of cancer. I was in Enterprise visiting one day and decided to stop by and see Mr. Morgan. He was Superintendent of Education at the time and was returning to his office. I had been talking with his Secretary Gladys Welch while he had gone down the hall. Gladys let him know I was there and he came down the hallway yelling and screaming, "Platt, get your rear end back here; we need to talk about those unruly kids of yours in the system – I'm tired of dealing with them and am not going to deal with them any longer!"

There was a problem. My kids were enrolled in a private school in Dothan at the time. This verbal "altercation" occurred while two sets of parents were waiting outside his office to see him. As we got to his office, he embraced me and we both shed a few tears. He was glad to see me, and I was glad to see him.

I can tell several funny stories about Mr. Morgan, but let's cut to the chase. In my chosen profession of television and radio, I have met a lot of educators. I have witnessed and been into several school systems throughout the states of Georgia, Florida, and Alabama. Make no mistake about it. There's never been a man to influence positively thousands of students whom Thad Morgan did during his career. There will never be another.

Thad Morgan, thank you for the influence in my life through all mistakes and everything I did wrong from time to time. I was always reminded I had someone who cared about me as you did for thousands of others.

School Board Members

Walt Wilkerson

Hillcrest Elementary was in the process of having maintenance on its building during the summer period. Superintendent Thad Morgan was driving by the school located on E. Watts Street and observed some people on the roof of the building. During this time Hillcrest school was experiencing some vandalism at the school. Superintendent Morgan became fixed on the individuals on the roof, thinking they might be vandals to the point he apparently forgot he was driving a car, lost control and drove the vehicle into a house located across from Hillcrest school. He picked up the name "Crash Morgan!"

At one school board meeting Bob Tomberlin, the Director of Transportation, presented a report on the need for additional three buses for the school system. Bob ended his presentation stating, "I am going to buy three new buses."

As Bob ended his report, Superintendent Morgan asked, "Mr. Tomberlin, what did you say?"

Bob replied, "I am going to buy three new buses."

Thad replied, "Mr. Tomberlin, I have told you multiple times that you can't buy anything. Only the Board can buy something. You can make a recommendation to the Board, but only the Board can act. Mr. Tomberlin, if you do not understand that, I can replace you with someone who understands it. Do you wish to amend your statement to the Board?"

Bob said, "Yes sir, I recommend that the Board purchase three new buses."

At the Board meeting that evening in the kitchen where refreshments were served, Bob Tomberlin said to Thad, "Mr. Morgan, I have a question for you. When you drove your car in front of Hillcrest school and stepped out of your car in that lady's living room, what did you say to her?"

"Tomberlin, you can ****######&&&&!!!"

Hugh Williams was Principal of Hillcrest Elementary School, and by all accounts was a good principal. Thad always referred to Hugh as the 13th best principal in the Enterprise system (the school only had 12 schools). Hugh on many occasions in meetings with the Superintendent, would state something like "Well, when I was in Montgomery, we didn't do it this way." Thad would then tell Hugh that was Montgomery, not Enterprise, and that if he wanted to go back to Montgomery, he would help arrange his return.

Hugh was always intimidated by Thad. He made the remark that he was mowing his lawn one Saturday morning and saw Thad drive by his house. Hugh said that he was intimidated and hoped Thad would not stop and get onto him about something so he just looked down and kept mowing. Hugh said that after Thad had driven by his house, he stopped mowing and threw up in his front yard.

One time, Thad, Bob, and Jimbo Reese walked over to Hillcrest when remodeling was going on. After the three of them entered the building, Thad went down the hall to the left and Bob and Jimbo stopped. Hugh came down the hall and saw those two but not Thad. Hugh said something like, "Where is the other *******?"

Thad was just turning the corner as Hugh spoke and said, "Here I am, Mr. Williams!"

The rest is history.

At the May 1985 Board meeting Dr. Bob Phares addressed the Board and gave a detailed report on the ACT, SAT, and California Achievement Tests for the year just ended. The report lasted 10-12 minutes and provided how the Enterprise System ranked both State and Nationally. After his report Bob asked if there were any questions.

Thad replied, "Dr. Phares, I understood everything in your report, but there were a lot of numbers in your report so you might want to repeat some of them for the people here."

Thad's tone at times could be intimidating, and Dr. Phares appeared to be a little shaken by Thad's statement. Bob slowly adjusted his tie, cleared his throat, and replied, "Mr. Morgan, if you understood everything, then everyone in this room understood it."

The Board and the room erupted in laughter. Thad then pointed his index finger at Dr. Phares and replied, "Phares, (not the respectful *Dr. Phares* when Thad called on him for his report), I brought your a** from Mississippi, and I can send it back just as quick."

At a football practice in the mid 1990s Thad pulled up in the school system car to watch practice. When he turned off the car, it continued to rumble and knock as some did at that time. It continued to rumble and knock for some 10-15 seconds before it finally quit. Dennis Johnson, head of maintenance for the school vehicles and by all accounts the yellow school buses that were well maintained, was at practice that day.

After the car finally quit knocking, Thad looked at Dennis and said, "If we had a decent maintenance supervisor, that vehicle would not do that. I guess if we painted it yellow, you could keep it in good working condition."

Dennis looked at Thad and replied, "It doesn't matter what color that car's painted. When cars are driven into people's homes, no one can maintain one treated like that."

Thad's reply can't be repeated in print.

Maxie Searcy was in a meeting in Montgomery, Alabama, and ran into Carl Stephens, Sports Director at WSFA TV. They discussed multiple sports stories. Carl asked Maxie where he was from, and Maxie replied, "Enterprise."

Carl said, "Enterprise? Y'all had that kooky principal who ran up and down the sidelines during football games challenging the officials and coaching the players. Whatever happened to that guy?"

Maxie thought for a minute about how to respond and then with some apprehension replied, "We made him Superintendent of Education!"

Jimmy Jones

There is one absolute truth regarding Mr. Morgan – he was proud of and loved the Enterprise School System. His dedication was evident at all times. I worked very closely with him for about eight years. Five of those years were as an Enterprise School Board member while he was Superintendent and the other three years while he served as a consultant assisting in the building of the new Enterprise High School. His dedication never wavered. I'm thankful for Mr. Morgan's friendship, his dedication, and the love he poured into this community.

Mary Alice Townsend

Where do I start talking about Thad Morgan? When I was appointed to the Enterprise City Board of Education, I was a young mother taking a break from teaching to stay home with our children. The oldest son had just started kindergarten in the school system. Son #2 would start school the next year.

I knew Thad Morgan by reputation - I must add a very big and complex local reputation. I had no real idea what I was getting into. Very simply, I saw it as an opportunity to give back to the community I had come to love and stay in touch with "education" on a new level. Those were my "personal agendas" as Thad called them.

I do not have one story or event, serious or comical, to share. There were many that would be viewed by each of you differently according to your perspective of the man. However, I do have two things that I would want everyone to understand from my perspective working with him as a member of the school board.

I never doubted Thad's love for the City of Enterprise or his love for the students who came through the doors of the schools in our city. I also saw those qualities later as I completed 19 years of teaching in the Enterprise City School System. Thad's influence, along with the influence of the good people he surrounded himself with, will continue to be felt as each school year begins and ends. His legacy, from my perspective, will always be his love for Enterprise and its students. He cared deeply and did it "his way"!

Len Sparks

A Hard Case with a Heart of Gold

Thank you, Jimbo, for the privilege to be included in this collection of stories. In my opinion Thad Morgan was a local hero and the man who set Enterprise Schools on the path from which it leads across the state today.

As an Enterprise transplant, marrying into the Enterprise family so to speak, Mr. Morgan's reputation preceded him. Mr. Morgan was Principal of Enterprise High School when my wife Nancy attended. Nancy had shared stories of Mr. Morgan catching students, boys and girls, in the hallways without a hall pass and giving them licks (paddlings). Who knew, a man before his time in gender equality!

I also have a couple of friends who were football players at the time and shared how they would do their best to dodge Mr. Morgan on his campus patrols but ultimately would be caught and suffer the wrath of his board. Not mentioning names but "Jip" and "Maddox" I'm sure deserved all he gave them. Those two and many others were molded literally and figuratively into upstanding adults who individually and collectively share a bond with this Man, A Hard Case with a Heart of Gold.

I have two stories I would like to share that in my opinion sum up Thad Morgan. The year was 2007 and we, the citizens of Enterprise, experienced a once in a lifetime event that changed us forever.

THE TORNADO!

I was serving as School Board President at the time and had seen Thad and talked with frequently and always at our monthly board meetings. Although retired, Thad was still very interested in the school system and enjoyed being around all the school administrators whom he had hired and mentored over the years.

During the aftermath of the tornado as we grieved the loss of Katie, Jamie, P.J., Michael, Michelle, A.J., Ryan, Mikey, and Mrs. Strickland, we began the difficult process of moving forward. What were we supposed to do next when there were so many questions to be answered? The feeling I had, and I feel that was shared by each of us, was that whatever we did it would impact generations to come, and it better be right.

Due to Alabama state laws on school construction at the time we were forced to relocate the high school to a location that had sufficient acreage to accommodate the buildings and grounds to be built that would enroll and educate over 2,000 Enterprise students.

During this process the Board hired Thad as consultant with his focus initially being on land procurement. As Jimbo, Bob, Rick, others and I traveled over Alabama and North Florida looking at schools and to Montgomery for funds, Thad was literally beating the bushes for that right piece of property.

As the choices were narrowed down, the present sight rose to the top like cream in a milk churn. Thad had come through with flying colors. However, there was one catch - the property was owned by two older brothers and like a lot of siblings, and especially older ones, it seemed they didn't agree on anything, much less selling their property.

Talking to different folks in the community, the consensus was that we should start looking for another site for the school because it would take a miracle for the two brothers to come together and agree to sell their property. Thad however was not discouraged and after several weeks of meeting with the brothers, he brokered a deal for the land that is now the home of Enterprise High School. The school includes the Performing Arts Center as well as the athletic venues and is regarded throughout the state of Alabama as the epitome of new high school construction.

I am convinced we would never have been able to purchase the property without Thad. The Hard Case, with the Golden Heart, influenced the two old brothers to agree on something that was bigger than the both of them and in doing so will be recognized forever as being the catalyst that brought the high school to realization.

My second story about Thad was told to me by my friend Herman, but his version was all about Thad. I wanted the rest of the story so I asked Thad about it, and he gave me his version which was all about Herman. Both men shared the same story but refrained from being the center of attention and only shared about the other. I now know the whole story so here it is.

It was in the early 60s and Thad had just arrived back in the county as Head Football Coach at Coffee Springs. Being originally from Enterprise and having a successful coaching career thus far, his reputation had preceded him. To hear Herman tell it they were scared to death of him but would have followed him into a fire wearing gasoline clothes.

Herman was a small scrappy young man and played line for Thad. Herman weighed 139 pounds pads and all. A wiry and gutsy young man with a heart as big as he was, Herman was just the kind of player Thad wanted to coach and be on his team, and the feeling was mutual. Herman loved playing football and especially for Thad. As the season was rocking along and all was going well, one Monday Herman didn't show up for practice. When Thad inquired about Herman's whereabouts, everyone said Herman had quit the team.

Thad knew something was wrong so after closing for the day and locking up, Thad headed straight to Herman's house to get to the bottom of the story. Thad arrived and was greeted by Herman's mother and was offered a glass of sweet tea. As Thad stood there in the yard sipping on his sweet tea, Herman's mother explained that the family was going through some tough times and as bad as she hated Herman having to quit the team, it just came to the point where he had to get a job and help the family make ends meet.

On this side of heaven we'll never know all the details as both Herman and Thad have gone to be with the Lord, but miraculously it worked out that Herman was back playing football and his job was accommodating his football. Herman always had a special place in his heart for Thad for organizing things so he could continue playing ball and still help his family.

The Hard Case, with a Heart of Gold, always had a special place in his heart for underdog in his life. Since his death there are literally hundreds of Herman stories that have been shared of how Thad over the years, with anonymity, stepped in and helped the less fortunate students through the trials of life.

Thad Morgan, you were a Hard Case, but you did, like it or not, have a Heart of Gold and for those of us on our journey through life and crossed paths with you, we are better for the meeting.

"Coach Morgan"

Andy Shelton

I am a member of the Enterprise High School Class of 1973. There are many stories of Mr. Morgan and his paddle. These two are special to me.

In the early 1970s Mr. Morgan was assistant football coach, track coach, P.E. and Drivers Education Teacher at EHS. Before the auxiliary gym was built behind the original gym, there were some old tennis courts. This area was designated as the official smoking area for students who had parental approval. Adjacent to the tennis courts was the football field house. The parking lot between Bates Memorial Stadium and the football practice field was used mostly by students.

Sometimes, daring students would try to leave football practice early by walking out the back door of the gym, across the tennis courts in front of the field house to get to their car in this parking lot. On some days Mr. Morgan would take up guard at the door of the field house waiting for these students who tried to leave early. In most cases a crowd would gather there at the field house to watch. Most of the skippers got all the way down the steps before realizing they were caught. Other and wiser students would ease the gym door open and stick their head out to see if the coast was clear. Regardless of their tactics, all would receive "licks" for their actions.

After graduation I attended college at Auburn University. During a break between quarters, I went by the high school to see Mr. Morgan. By this time he was the Principal at EHS. I entered the office to be greeted by his secretary Ms. Gladys Welch. She asked if she could help me, and I replied I would like to see Mr. Morgan. She replied he was in a meeting, but I could wait if I liked.

Mr. Morgan's office was adjacent to the area I was to wait in. I could hear Mr. Morgan in a spirited conversation with a student's parents regarding his unruly behavior. I could lean over the counter between Mrs. Welch and me and see Mr. Morgan at his desk. After a minute or so Mr. Morgan looked out and saw me waiting, and in mid-sentence he barked "What do you want, Andrew?"

I replied quickly, "I came by to get some medicine, Mr. Morgan."

He looked back at the parents and said, "Give me one minute." He retrieved his paddle, met me at the door, and delivered a sharp lick to my rear end. When I turned to leave, I looked into his office at the parents sitting there with their mouths open wide.

I said, "Thank you, Sir."

Mr. Morgan's paddle had a dual role. Not only did it dispense much needed discipline, but it also built many fond memorable relationships.

After I finished college, I was blessed to be able to return home with my wife, Debbie Watson Shelton. Deb was hired to teach school in Enterprise by Mr. Morgan in 1987. In my job as an engineer with the Alabama Power Company I had many opportunities to work with Mr. Morgan when existing schools were renovated and new schools were built. I also got to work with him when the new Hillcrest Elementary School and the new Enterprise High School were built after the 2007 tornado. By this time Mr. Morgan was retired, but his love for Enterprise City Schools never ended.

Bill Foreman

THE WEATHERMAN

"As Best I Recall"

Enterprise football practices in the late 1960s and early 1970s were as much of a survival as they were a training methodology. At Enterprise Junior High in 1969 Coach Thad Morgan made sure that they were tough and that only the strong survived. For instance, there were NO water breaks, and we went full contact, full speed *Everyday* – except the day before a game. Monday practices were always the worst of the lot.

One Monday, early in the 1969 season, it was raining hard – kind of rain known as a "frog strangler." Those of us on the EJHS football team that year just knew we would not be able to practice outside that day – not because it was raining – that would not have stopped practice – but because the rain was accompanied by serious lightning. All day long when we checked the weather outside, we would secretly grin knowing that this storm would yield a much easier practice in the gym. There were no covered Astroturf practice fields back then. Plus, by this time of the year, we had long since destroyed any grass on our practice field. So, it was now just a sanctuary for dirt, which would be a big ole mud pit on this rainy afternoon.

Well, finally the end of the school day came, and we dutifully filed into the locker room to begin changing into our practice gear – all with a sense of relief that we would be spared at least this one Monday practice.

Just as were getting our gear out of our lockers, Coach Morgan entered the locker room and in his booming voice announced, "Y'all get dressed – full pads – I done turned the water off!!" Now these were by no means scattered showers. Now, it had been raining, and I remind you, lightning all day. Surely it was not going to stop now – besides, he can't do that, can he!?

We slowly finished dressing out in full pads and filed out into the covered walkway to for wait what we prayerfully hoped would be light-weight practice in the gym. To our dismay, the lightning started subsiding and then to our horror, the rain began to slow; and what made it even worse was the fact that some brave (or more likely "unenlightened") souls had snickered, out loud, when Coach made his announcement.

Then the clouds broke, and the sun came out on that muddy excuse for a practice field. Now not only would we be soaking wet but dealing with the extreme humidity that only those in the Deep South who have endured it can appreciate. Those of us on that 1969 EJHS team became believers. As things worked out, we would go on to play with Coach Morgan's "robust encouragement" for the rest of our years in Wildcat Blue. But we never doubted his words again. Don't know how it happened, but it did – just the way I've told it – in this here story.

ASSUME THE POSITION

"As Best I Recall"

Discipline at Enterprise High School in the early 1970s was an expectation for ALL students. Two Assistant Principals/Coaches, Coach Morgan and Coach Peavy happily administered those expectations. Coach Peavy was a very large but relatively quiet black man who took care of any black students who needed a session with his "board of education." Now back in those days this Board of Education was not a group of people listening attentively to you plead your case as it might be today. No, this was a real wooden board - more commonly known as a "paddle."

Coach Morgan, on the other hand, was the very loud, boisterous and demanding white man who happily doled out the "Medicine," as he called it, to any would-be-trouble-makers who happened to be of the Caucasian variety. His "paddle" was actually a baseball bat that had been planed down on one side and had holes drilled through for extra "effectiveness" at impact. The purpose of this "instrument of correction" was to leave an impression on the buttock of any offending youth. I might add, from personal experience, that it produced the desired "result."

Now if you happened to be an EHS athlete who played football, and especially if you were a member of the offensive or defensive line, you would get some additional "extra-special attention" from Coach Morgan. As a linebacker and sometimes center, I was a member of this extra special attention getting group.

I remember one day walking down the hall minding my own

business, and suddenly without warning, I hear an all too familiar voice yell out, "Foreman!" I, of course, immediately halted my forward progress, turned around, and responded with "Yes Sir, Coach Morgan."

"Have you had your medicine today?" Coach thundered back.

For those of you uninitiated souls reading this narrative, there was no right answer to this question when posed by Coach Morgan.

If you said "Yes Sir," he would say something like "Good, I'm glad I ran into you. You obviously didn't get enough to do you any good."

On the other hand, if you responded in the negative, as in "No Sir," then he'd say something to the effect "Well, today is your lucky day. I just happen to have the medicine you need here in my hand."

Next came the words you knew were coming. "Assume the position!"

"But Coach I haven't done anything."

He would say, "Foreman, I know you've done something...I just ain't caught you yet...now "Assume the Position!" Again, for the uninitiated, I'll translate that command. "Assume the Position" meant "Grab your ankles and kiss your a** goodbye," whereupon you would receive your MEDICINE in the form of a sound lick with his aforementioned paddle. Unfortunately, on this particular occasion,

I neglected to thank Coach Morgan for my medicine so he administered another dose to help me remember the "Thank You" for the next such occasion.

Now to be completely fair, these "I just ain't caught you yet" licks were what he called "Love Taps." However, they did sting. But they were nothing like the butt lifting, impression leaving Whacks you'd receive for a felonious transgression of the rules and expectations. I should also add, to my knowledge, no one ever lost life or limb from these paddlings although some came pretty close to losing another part of their anatomy - and I know of at least a few guys whose lives were probably turned around due to Coach Morgan's type of medicine.

I do recall another humorous adjunct to this story involving two students – I'll call them "Howard' and "Otis" after two similar type characters on the old *Andy Griffith Show*.

The name "Howard" was selected based on the fictional character Howard Sprague who was Mayberry's town accountant. He always wore a bow tie and coat every day. He was very proper and polite, seldom raising his voice. This Mayberry Howard is similar to the "Howard" in our story in that neither one would ever have expected to get into anything close enough trouble to end up in Coach Morgan's office in need of some medicine.

Now as you may recall, Mayberry's "Otis" was always a frequent guest in the town jail. He would let himself in "his" jail cell – cell #2. Well, as you might have guessed, our EHS student "Otis" was well acquainted with the path to the office as well as Coach Morgan's board of education that he knew all too well.

Anyway, on this particular day Howard and Otis were both waiting outside Coach Morgan's office (aka "The Sanctuary of Discontent") as Coach returned from a meeting. He was not in a good mood.

As Coach Morgan opened the door to his office, he shouted back to the two offenders, "Who's first?"

Howard had actually arrived first so he meekly offered, "I guess I am." As he timidly stepped into the sanctuary of discontent, Coach Morgan bellowed, "Assume the Position!" Now, Howard, having heretofore never been to the school office for anything other than to pick up some type of academic award or certificate of achievement, had never heard those words before. He just stood there with that deer-in-the-headlights look – having no idea what was being required of them.

Now Otis, as a regular offender, stepped around Howard, bent down, and grabbed the ankles and said, "Here, let me show you how to do this!" This was followed by a large whacking sound and then quickly by a loud grunting noise as Otis received his just wages for his previously offending actions.

Howard, after receiving this "education by example" from Otis, dutifully bent down and grabbed his ankles and received his just desserts as well. As I recall, Howard was never again seen in the Sanctuary of Discontent – proving once again that smart people learned from one such application.

Unlike our friend Otis.

BILL FOREMAN

CASTING THE VISION
"As Best I Recall"

It was a beautiful day in the fall of 1968 as we were nearing the end of a P.E. class with Coach Thad Morgan at the helm. I was in the 8th grade at Enterprise Junior High School along with a host of other guys who would play Enterprise football and eventually become known as "Thad's Boys" (which over time morphed into ThadZ-Boyz in deference to his lack of adherence to the use of the English vernacular). Oddly, Mrs. Janice Morgan, his wife, was a very elegant and proper teacher of the English Language in our school. A definite case of "opposites attract." But I digress... back to our 8th grade P.E. class.

Coach Morgan was sitting under a large oak tree in one of those old gray folding chairs – leaning back, as I recall. We, the members of the 8th grade P.E. class, were standing and listening intently as he began his monologue regarding his thoughts on how many games his teams should win. (Side note: even those in the class who were never going to play football were happily listening intently because if we were standing and listening, we were not running laps and huffing, puffing, and sweating).

"Most people say I'm greedy when it comes to winning football games," he began. "That's not true," he continued. "I just want to win our fair share of games. Now if we only play 5 games, we should win 5 games. That's our fair share. If we play 7 games, we should win 7. That's our fair share. If we play 10, we should win 10. Now let's say we play 15 games one season. What do you think is our share of that season – 10, 12, 14? Heck no, if we play 100 we should win 100. That's our share! I'm not greedy! I just want to win our fair share."

Thadz Boyz, many of whom were in that 8th grade P.E. class that day, ended up under Coach Morgan's motivational leadership producing a stellar set of years in the history of Enterprise football. During our 5 years of football seasons from our 8th grade through 12th grades at EJHS and EHS, we had 3 undefeated and untied seasons, and in our senior season in 1972, we became the first Enterprise team to go to the state playoffs. Back then, for us to get into the playoffs required us to have an undefeated season. (Only 8 teams from each of the 4 divisions could go to the playoffs back then). When it was all over, we had lost only 4 games in our 5 years as Autumn Warriors for the City of Enterprise.

Years later, as I was pursuing a graduate degree in Business Management, one of the topics covered under the category of Motivational Leadership was that of "Casting the Vision and Setting Expectations." My mind ran back to that day in 1968 under that huge oak tree at EJHS with Coach Morgan's booming voice talking about winning Enterprise's share of football games. I realized at that moment that Coach Morgan, knowing that many of us in that P.E. class were going to be a big part of the Enterprise football teams of the coming years, was doing that – Setting Expectations and Casting His Vision for success on the gridiron and in life after our playing days were done. Funny I don't remember him having an MBA...but based on the results outlined herein, I'd say he did a pretty darn good job. WOULDN'T YOU? GO BIG BLUE!

*Notes: For the historians in the audience, those 5 years were:

1968 – EJHS 7-0-0 Coach Morgan was the Head Coach

1969 - EJHS 7-0-0 Coach Morgan was the Head Coach

1970 - EHS Jr. Varsity (AKA "B" Team) 8-1 Coach Morgan was the Head Coach of the "B" Team

1971 - EHS Varsity 8-2-0 Coach Paul Terry was Head Coach and Coach Morgan was Asst. Head Coach

1972 - EHS Varsity 10-0-0 plus 1 loss in Quarter Finals of State Championship Playoffs (Coach Terry was Head Coach and Coach Morgan was Asst. Head Coach)

"FROM 0-10 to 10-0-0"

"AS BEST I RECALL"

Some fellow named Chuck Dickens (I think he was from over around ~~Andyilusia,~~ ~~Andialoosa,~~ Opp) wrote a book *A Tale of Two Cities*. This story, which by contrast, is a true one, could be called *A Tale of Two Turning Points*.

The 1972 football season for Enterprise High ended up as "one for the books." It was an almost magical undefeated and untied 10-0-0 regular season followed by Enterprise's first ever trip to the recently established state playoff system.

But at the half-time of only our third game of that season, we were BEHIND... and by two scores – 10 to zero! Up until this moment, as recounted elsewhere in this book, this group of seniors had only suffered 3 losses in our careers - going back to the 8th grade at EJHS - and only one of those losses was by more than 2 points and none more than 1 score. So being behind as seniors and starters by 10 at the half was unprecedented for this group. Enterprise behind at the half by 10 points – why that was unheard of in that era. This was a crisis!

Now, the team we were playing that night was no slouch. We were playing Auburn High. And if my memory serves me correctly, they entered the game that night undefeated and ranked number 3 in the state. Usually, our half-times were comfortable affairs with us ahead. They were non-emotional moments spent refreshing ourselves for the 2nd half and making minor adjustments to our alignments and the details of how we were lining up or blocking, attacking, blitzing, etc.

But this was different. WE WERE BEHIND and we hadn't even scored! We dutifully filed into our locker room, got some water, and sat down as always waiting for our coaches to emerge to make the above-mentioned changes. To our surprise, none of the Coaches were with us in the locker room. They were all sitting in the Coaches office behind closed doors. Years later we found out that, by not immediately coming into the locker room, their plan was to use some version of reverse psychology on us.

Anyway, as the seconds trickled by into minutes an uneasy silence filled the locker room. Tick... Tick... Tick... Tick... And then suddenly from the Coaches Office, without warning, we heard a commotion that sounded like a young war. We heard something being thrown against the door, followed by some loud bellowing. We heard the audible words of "I can't stand it!!" preceded and followed by some "expletives."

It was the distinctive sound of a Coach Morgan's angry voice - not unlike what you might expect to hear from a hungry Grizzly Bear emerging from a long hibernation. This was immediately followed by the sound of the door to the Coaches office being flung open and crashing into the wall as if it was a runaway freight train.

Instantly, it seems, Coach Morgan emerged from the office and appeared in the Locker Room where we were all seated in anxious anticipation - mixed with dread. His face was so filled with rage that it seemed to glow hot red. Had he been a cartoon character, his ears would have had smoke bellowing out of them and his head would have been exploding. The sophomores and juniors on our team sat there with astonished looks on their faces. But for those of us who were seniors... we had seen this "Mad Thad" look one time before and had hoped to never see it again.

Now, for the reader to understand the full impact of the following account of what actually happened, I must retreat in time by 2 seasons – back to the fall of 1970. Those of us that were seniors in 1972 were sophomores during the 1970 season, and as such, we played mostly in just the "B Team" games that year. That 1970 "B Team" had an excellent year - experiencing only a single loss by a single point to one of the top teams in the state at that time. However, the Varsity Team of 1970 had a "seldom-experienced-by-Enterprise" losing season, posting only a 4-5-1 record that year.

Toward the end of the 1970 Varsity season, we traveled to Crampton Bowl in Montgomery to play Jeff Davis – a highly regarded team in the state during those early years of the

1970s. Although most of us on that 1970 "B Team" were not expecting to enter this game, we traveled as members of the Varsity team - primarily as back-up players in case of injury to one of the starters. At half-time of that game we were behind by a reasonably recoupable score of 13-6. So, there was no call for half-time drama. We made adjustments, received the normal "we can win this one" speeches from our coaches and summarily returned to the field of battle for what we hoped would be a proud turning point from a then disappointing season to a respectable one.

However, the second half for us was a complete disaster. By the fourth quarter we appeared to have given up and just quit trying altogether. We got beat. And I mean we got beat BAD - losing 47 to 6, which meant we gave up 34 points and scored NONE in the second half of that game. It was a total collapse of spirit. I don't recall much being said by the coaches after that game. But I can tell you it was a long, long, long, bus ride back to the home of the Boll Weevil monument.

With much dread, Monday came. We heard rumors of a "Rededication Program" coming our way at football practice that afternoon. We didn't know what that was, but it clearly did NOT sound like an enjoyable experience.

As practice started, we heard alarming foreshadowing words coming from our coaches. Those of us that had grown up with Coach Morgan since our Junior high days, knew that when we heard Coach Morgan saying things like: "You better buckle your chin strap" and "Today we gonna find out who-is-and-who-ain't, who-can-and-who-can't, who-will-and-who-won't" – it was going to be a particularly grueling practice session fraught with intense physical exertion and, in the case of football practice - excessive "collisions".

We were not disappointed. That afternoon's practice seemed to go on forever. As on all Mondays we were in full pads and had a full contact, full speed practice. Then after the normal game week practice, we entered a series of seemingly endless but varying hitting drills. After that, we lined up and ran sprints 'til our lungs, it seemed, were ready to burst. But since sprints usually signaled the approaching end of practice, we thought that we might just survive. Besides, it was getting dark.

However, our fleeting hopes of "a reprieve by darkness" were soon dashed, when after "25 of each," the limited lighting we had on the practice field back then was turned "on." Additionally, cars were lined up with their head lights shining on the field to supplement the dim glow of the practice field lights - all so that we could continue our rededication program.

Next, we were directed to "circle up" for some "Root-Hoggin." Now, "Root-Hoggin," which, next to "THE CAGE," was one of Coach Morgan's favorite drills. It is a one-on-one affair in which each of the two reluctant participants line up "on all fours." Each player positions his head under the shoulder of his opponent. On Coach's sound, the two "root-hoggers" start trying desperately to push each other out of the "circle." The ensuing awkward linear struggle continues between the two until Coach Morgan deems it ended by the second sound of his voice. Now, while this exercise doesn't sound too bad, it is totally exhausting, especially to the already tired legs of the contestants on that particular day. After we "root-hogged" for a while, we lined up for sprints – again. Then 25 more. Surely, this would be the end of the practice that seemed to have no end. But, "NO," we were directed to another round of futile and purposefully fatiguing drills. Finally, and oh so thankfully, it ended, and we wearily summoned our last ounce of energy to at least appear to be running off of the practice field.

It was worse the first day of spring training – which was as much for weeding out "those who ain't" as it was for teaching those "who is" about the "X's and O's." But this was in the middle of the season with a game this coming Friday. Surely, tomorrow won't be this bad again - we hoped.

Oh, how quickly Tuesday afternoon cycled around. Day two of our rededication program, believe it or not, was worse than day one – or a at least it seemed that way to my overworked and aching body parts. Wednesday followed the same tortuous pattern. We survived, but never forgot that "rededication program," as Coach Morgan termed it.

So, with that backdrop, the reader will understand our apprehension as we looked upon another red-faced Coach Morgan (quietly and somewhat reverentially known as "Mad Thad") as our story of "Half-time of the 1972 Auburn game" continues.

Now every good football team has to have good offensive and defensive lines. And every good line, whether it be offensive or defensive, has to be anchored by two good tackles as they form, in essence, the foundation of the team. That year we were blessed to have two GREAT tackles – Ben Parrish and Jim Mims. And in contrast to the dawning era of two-platoon football, these two guys were still playing both ways – offense and defense – which means they literally never came off the field of battle unless we were ahead, or they were injured.

That reality meant they were constantly playing across from a guy that had been resting for half of the game. Especially, during the fourth quarter, they would be exhausted while they were continuingly battling an intermittently rested opponent. So, as Coach Morgan would say it: "you-can-bet-your-mama's-egg-money" that these two fine tackles were not slackers on the field of competition.

Anyway, back to our story. The first thing I remember Coach Morgan shouting as he exploded into the locker room was "That was the most piss-pour crap I've ever seen from y'all." Then he saw that Ben and Jim were sitting right next to each other. He marched over and grabbed each one of them by their shoulder pads and jammed the two of them together as if they were bowling pins.

At the same time, he was thundering back at all of us: "Now, y'all go out there and lay your sorry a**es around in the second half like you did in the first half, and I'll kick all your a**es to Daleville and back next week!!! " This was his delicate way of "promising" us another rededication program - if we failed to win this game. This subtle point was not lost on those of us that had actually experienced such a program.

Then he wheeled completely around 180 degrees to glare directly at me and said "Foreman, damnit!- get both hands up next time!" He was referring to the fact that during the first half, I had failed to intercept a pass that he thought I should have made. On the positive side, I had knocked down the pass down. Although the reason I didn't get both hands up was due to the fact that I was off balance as I was being "illegally engaged" around my feet at that moment by an opponent.

I prudently decided, in a nano-second, not to plead this fact in my defense to Coach Morgan in that particular moment in time. I decided instead to respond with a simple but hearty "Yes, Sir," so as not to attract any more of his anger in my direction. That way he could move on to others in the room – like maybe Sam Pickett, Bruce Heath, or Bob Layton. I figured that they might also benefit from his performance improving "suggestions." I'm not a greedy individual - no use in me hoggin' the spotlight and becoming an example for future references.

Well, by the end of this, seemingly-never-ending half-time, we were sufficiently persuaded that in the paraphrased words of John Heisman "it would have been better for each of us to have died as a small boy than to fail to go back out there and win this game."

We went back out the second half, played like our lives were on the line ('cause they were!) and won the game 13-10. Looking back, that half-time was THE Turning Point for that season. We were never behind at half time again and we went on to achieve the rarely experienced perfect 10-0-0 regular season that year.

Later in my business career, I came to the realization that being an effective leader of people in any endeavor – whether a company, a church, or a football team is as much psychology as it is strategy. Coach Morgan, as it turned out, was quite the psychologist.

He knew us and knew us well. For some of us, this was the fifth year of football under his watchful, disciplinarian eye. He knew what we were capable of doing and he knew when we were not playing up to those capabilities. He knew how to motivate us, and he had demonstrated the willingness to use harsh disciplinary practices to "cure" any "perceived deficiencies" in our performances.

Personally, I don't think that the Coaches' original "reverse psychology" plan would have achieved the same results that night. Besides, I didn't even think we were playing all that poorly during the first half of the Auburn Game that night. But... my mind was changed, and by the time I left that locker room and hit the field for the second half, I was both convinced and properly motivated to play harder than ever for the remainder of that contest. I have never before or since felt that eager to get out of a locker room and back on the field to hit somebody – anybody.

Coach Morgan may not have been a licensed psychologist, but he knew how to use the tools of his trade to motivate us better, I believe, than anyone with such a license. We never again had to have another one of those sessions facing "Mad Thad" and his version "direct" psychology. This was "THE Turning Point" in that memorable and glorious season and, for many of us in that room, a tough point in our lives during those times when things were not going well in our individual journeys through time.

As I write these lines, it is August of 2023. Dawn is breaking on a new day. The steady Tick, Tock, Tick, Tock of my grandfather clock reminds me that time is marching on. I'm now 68 years old. I was 17 when we played Auburn that night at Bates Memorial Stadium. Coach Morgan passed on into the eternity beyond this past March – just days shy of his 85th birthday. A lifetime has transpired since that half-time "chat" – my life-time. Kinda makes one stop and think.

There is something more about that half-time "conversation" that I've missed in my recounting above - something deeper. Yes, we were fearful of facing another rededication program had we lost. But there is more to it than just that.

I realize now that Coach Morgan was truly invested in us and our success – both on the field and off. In today's jargon, "he was all in." And somewhere deep inside we knew that, and we didn't want him to be disappointed in us. That's why we responded so enthusiastically and won that game. He knew that those of us sitting in that locker room that night had the potential to have a great season – even a legacy season. And he knew that losing this game - a game he could see that we clearly had the capabilities of winning, would derail that great season. We might still have had a good season, but it would not have been the legacy season it became.

So... Thanks, Coach. Thanks for pouring so abundantly of yourself into our lives. It has made us better in every way. We miss you, Coach. We love you, Coach.

Jim Mims

I am truly honored to have the opportunity to share a few of my experiences and memories of Coach Morgan. Most people refer to him as "Thad" or "Mr. Morgan" and know him from his role as Principal or Superintendent. But to those who played for him or were in school while he was coaching will always be known as "Coach Morgan." He was a very complex man that could be tough as nails and demand perfection from athletes. But once you peeled back that gruff exterior, he was a very caring person who was much more concerned with building character than he was with training athletes.

Outside of my father, Coach Morgan had a more significant impact on my life than any other man. That impact is still felt today. I suspect many people could fill an entire book with their recollections of Coach Morgan, as I know he impacted many people during his lifetime. I will briefly share a few of mine.

I was first introduced to Coach Morgan in the 7th grade at Enterprise Junior High School (affectionately known as "Old Junior High"). His reputation had already filtered down to us 6th graders at the nearby College Street Elementary School the previous year. We had heard how stern and tough he was in PE class and that he made athletes run until they dropped. We even heard that if they lost a football game at Coffee Springs, he kept the stadium lights on and made them practice after the game! (We later learned that these rumors were all, in fact, true). So, by the time I started 7th grade, I was already intimidated by him even though I had not met him.

During Jr High, I played football and basketball. Our football teams were undefeated (we'd heard the Coffee Springs rumors and didn't want the same experiences!), and our basketball teams didn't lose many games. We didn't always have the best athletes, but you could rest assured we were always more dis-ciplined, in better shape physically, and better prepared than our opponents. And you could bet your bottom dollar the word "quit" was not in our vocabulary!

The event from Jr High that stands out more than another occurred during 9th grade shortly after school began in the fall. We had been practicing football for several weeks before the beginning of school, and our first game wasn't for a few more weeks. For anyone growing up in South Alabama, it's not hard to visualize how miserable it was practicing during the sum-mer heat and humidity. But to truly understand our plight, you also need to understand our practice field behind the school was a combination of hard clay and sand interspersed with pebbles. We practiced in full pads and had very few water breaks. And throw in that we felt we were being drilled by Vince Lombardi (or Atila The Hun); describing the experience as somewhat miserable would be an understatement.

After one challenging day of practice, the thought of quitting crept into my mind. The next day during PE, I talked with another person with the same thoughts, and we decided to quit. At the end of PE, we informed Coach we were leaving the team. He scowled at us and told us to drop off our equipment in his office. The rest of the day, I kept second-guessing myself about quitting and felt horrible that I had made a mistake.

Late in the day, an announcement came over the intercom for me to report to Mr. Morgan's office. He is sitting at his desk, asks me to take a seat, and in a very calm voice, says, "Jim, you didn't want to quit, did you?" I responded that he was correct and that I didn't want to quit. He told me that was what he suspected; perhaps someone had talked me into it. I told him he was correct.

Coach Morgan told me that when someone quits, he rarely questions it, but he felt, in my case, he didn't feel like I wanted to. He then told me he had yet to put up my equipment and that I had to decide right then whether I wanted to play. He said to get my gear and put it in my locker if I wanted to play. I told him I did want to play and got up to get my equipment. As I was about to leave, he said, "Jim, now, don't ever quit on me again." I responded, "You can count on it!."

What I didn't realize at the time, his allowing me back on the team had very little to do with football . Several other players could have taken my spot on the team. But what Coach Morgan knew was if I quit, just because it was tough, then it would be easier to quit the next time things were tough. And then easier the next time. And before long, quitting could easily become a habit.

I remember three years later, during my senior year at EHS, we were undefeated in the regular season but lost in the playoffs. As I was walking off the field after that loss, I remembered back to that day when I tried to quit in Jr. High. I can assure you there were many times I wanted to quit football, but I had given him my word. After showering and dressing, as I was leaving the fieldhouse, he called me into the office, told me he remembered that day I tried to quit, and thanked me for keeping my word. He told me our entire team should hold our heads up because we were walking out as winners.

It still stung that we lost the game, but I found a new respect for Coach Morgan. Like many others, I have had tough times in life when I didn't think I could keep going. My sports experiences were a large part of the foundation and preparation for the tough times in later life. One of the big lessons I learned was regardless of the scoreboard, you only lose once you give up. The same is true in life. Thank you, Coach Morgan, for allowing me back on the team and teaching me never to give up!

Toward the end of the 9th-grade year, we were thinking about spring football over at the high school, and the thought did cross mine, and I'm sure others' minds that after three tough years, we would be leaving Coach Morgan behind, and life would become easier. Much to our surprise, we discovered that Coach Morgan was moving to high school with us! Lucky us! But those of us who spent those three years at EJHS and then moved up to EHS with Coach Morgan held a special place in his heart. He often referred to us as "His Boys." I now wear that badge proudly.

As we moved to high school Coach Morgan continued coaching, primarily the linemen, and became Assistant Principal. I could tell so many stories from those three years that picking a few is difficult. I will briefly discuss our football team and the season we had during our senior year. The fall of 1972 was a memorable season for our football team, student body, and the city.

Our team lost quite a few starters and some excellent athletes from the previous year, and many people felt this would be a rebuilding year. And to be candid, even though we had a few exceptional athletes (some who continued to play in college), our talent wasn't tremendously deep, considering the level of competition we would be playing. But there was something special about that group that molded together to be a team. Our coaching staff (Paul Terry, Coach Morgan, Ben Baker, and Larry Eddins) did a masterful job developing and preparing us. We went undefeated in the regular season for the first time in many years and made the state playoffs for the first time ever.

I want to mention some specific things that happened during that season. We began the season with two wins but didn't play particularly well in either of those games, and in some respects, we were fortunate to come out with wins. Our third game at home against Auburn High School was quite memorable in several respects, and in retrospect, the success of our season was on the line in this contest.

We came out the first half, and borrowing a term from Coach Morgan, we "Stunk up the Field"! We made mistake after mistake, and at halftime, Auburn was leading by the score of 10-0. As we ran off the field, one of the sophomores running beside me asked, "Do you think we have a chance to come back?" I responded, "We have them right where we want them!" After his puzzled look indicated he was probably questioning my sanity, I continued, "You've never been in a halftime with

Coach Morgan when we've been behind!"

I knew what was about to happen, and it would not be pretty. But I also knew the Wildcat team coming out of the locker room would be much different than the team that went in. I entered the locker room braced for the upcoming "fireside chat." Let's say Coach Morgan did not disappoint. The coaches were huddled in their office for a few moments, and then it broke loose. I won't repeat what was said as some of it is probably unsuitable. But we were appropriately reminded in no uncertain terms of how poorly we had played.

After the Coach Morgan vintage "Pep Talk," we came out of the locker room with a different outlook on life and a determination to redeem ourselves.

The first play from scrimmage set the tone for the rest of the game. We called a "Quick Pitch Left." As the Left Tackle, my job was to pull out in front of Bob Layton, the running back, and block a linebacker or cornerback. Bruce Heath was the Tight End and would block the Defensive End towards the inside. The ball was snapped, Bruce executed his block perfectly, and headed downfield, looking to block someone else. I pulled out like I'd done many times before, steamrolled one defender, and headed downfield to block another defender. Bob did an excellent job, and we gained about 12 or 13 yards on the play. After the play ends, Bob hops up off the ground, sticks his finger in one of the defender's faces, and says, "Yall's a**es are whipped!" Bruce and I are compelling Bob to get back in the huddle before we get a penalty! At that point, most of us knew that we weren't walking off the field without a W, and we didn't. I don't think Auburn even got another first down the entire game. Final score ENTERPRISE 13, AUBURN 10. That comeback win set the stage for the remainder of the season.

Ed.'s note – Bill Foreman also provided a vivid account of the EHS comeback win over Auburn High School (especially the halftime "fireworks") in his recollections that appear in this book.

Another humorous memory occurred after practice one day. I am in the locker room getting dressed. Someone rushes in and tells me I need to get outside because Coach Morgan hit my car as he was leaving the parking lot! Here we are after practice where he'd been yelling at me, and now, he hits my car! But any of you who knew him well knew that his driving skills could sometimes be suspect.

He was very apologetic and assured me he would fix it. The next day I DROVE HIM to his insurance agent's office to file a claim. His frustration soon turned to celebration as he discovered my insurance was with the same company, and he would have to pay no deductible. He was in a great mood on the way back to the school. But suffice to say, his great mood had soured when we began practice later that afternoon.

After high school and college, I moved away and only occasionally came back for a visit. I would go by for a visit when passing through. Coach Morgan was always excited to see me, and if he knew I was there, he stopped whatever he was doing and visited for as long as I would stay. He met my wife DeeDee and definitely approved of her. Whenever I saw or talked to him through the years, he always wanted to know how she was doing. He consistently told me (as I know he said to others) when I married her that I had "Outkicked my Coverage."

My wife has been a teacher and school administrator for many years, and whenever she was with me for a visit, the two of them would talk shop. Later as my wife started a Christian school in Texas, he gave us some excellent advice several times. Whenever I spoke with him in the last few years of his life, we discussed our school more than any other topic. He was always a huge encouragement.

He also enjoyed meeting my daughters, Jessica and Caitlin. It was a typical Coach Morgan experience when he met Caitlin, our youngest. Now when she was a toddler, she was a handful. She was a strong-willed drama queen that was always getting into something.

As we pulled out outside his office this particular day, I read the Riot Act to Caitlin (she was about three years old at the time) and told her she better be on her best behavior! We walked in, and when Coach Morgan realized we were there, he kicked some people out of his office and invited us in. We were all sitting on his famous "low-rider" couch. Caitlin couldn't sit still as we talked, and I attempted to corral her. So, she stood up and started messing with papers on his desk.

As I began to scold her, Coach Morgan shot me a dirty look, pointed at me, and with a voice reminiscent of a football practice field, said, "Jim, you leave her alone!" He then tells Caitlin, "Honey, come over here and sit in my lap. You can play with anything on my desk you want to!" I just looked at my wife and said, "I don't know this man!" We laugh about that story now, but I didn't think it was too funny then!

As the years rolled on, my discussions with Coach began to shift. We talked less about football and more about spiritual matters. He often would call me and ask me to pray for one of my teammates or coaches who were struggling. He asked me several times to pray for health concerns for him or a family member.

He was very secure in his salvation through Jesus Christ and wanted to make sure others he knew had that same assurance. As his health began to fail, he became more concerned about others' spiritual condition than his health.

I would always let him know when I would be in the area, and we would arrange a time for me to come by for a visit. He would often apologize in advance for not having much stamina. Our routine soon became that we would visit until he needed to rest. He never wanted to tell me he was tired but would say, "Jim, can you pray for us?" That would be my signal he was worn out. Even though he has passed into eternity, his impact on the world will live through everyone who knew him. Rest in Peace, Coach!

Bruce Heath

Thanks for the opportunity to say a word about Coach Morgan. He was not only the father figure in my life that he was to so many guys and girls, but he had a major influence on my life. I was one of the fortunate few who had Coach Morgan for six years as Coach and Assistant Principal.

He was a man's man, but he knew how to be tender when necessary and could say what he needed to say and you understood. I remember that he came to my father's funeral several years ago. It was the day after Thanksgiving and everybody had some place else to be, but he came to hug me and console me. He was so proud of us and had tremendous confidence in us.

One Friday night when I was an underclassman, the Enterprise eleven were getting whipped soundly and I heard Coach Morgan say to Coach Terry, "Coach, let me put my boys in there! They won't quit on you like this!"

(Ed.'s Note – Bruce was one of the players who had played for Thad three years when Thad was the Head Coach at EJHS.

The poem *Thanatopsis* says it well. Coach lived a good life and with an "unfaltering faith wrapped the drapery of his couch about him and lay down to silent dreams."

Sam Pickett

Jim Reese phoned me one day shortly after Coach passed and asked if I would write a few pages describing mine and Coach's relationship. My initial reaction was of intense reservation. How could I possibly describe this man who was my teacher, coach, mentor and very much a father figure.

I was once asked to speak at a Roast for both Coach Morgan and Coach Bacon. I was honored by the request, but I knew I could not possibly talk about Coach Morgan without speaking quite frankly in describing this complex man. Those of you who knew Coach and know Coach for his frank and straight forward speech understand that to properly describe Coach and the events one is attempting to portray, one must be able to use terms which are descriptive. There was no way I could do that in a mixed audience.

For example, if one were to ask me to describe Coach Bacon, I would tell a story of a time when I was attempting to recruit a player of his. I was a Graduate Assistant Coach at a small college and my Head Coach instructed me to ask Coach Bacon if the young man could read. With a serious face and his dead pan delivery, he stated, "I don't know if he can read a book, but he can read a guard." I understood immediately.

A similar story concerning Coach Morgan occurred when I was a junior at Enterprise High School. After a talent show and during mid-morning break there was an altercation in the smoking area. Coach Morgan and Coach Peavy came out and Coach Morgan simply stated to me, "Take one more step Pickett, and I will give you your walking papers." Simply stated but clearly understood.

There was no altercation.

Coach Morgan served as a teacher, coach, assistant principal, principal, and superintendent during a time when local communities and states still had control of their school systems – a time of rules, guidelines, and standards when education was based on merit and personal achievement. Needless to say, Enterprise had students who graduated and continued their education at universities throughout the country with tremendous success. However, Enterprise and its educational leadership and faculty believed in a common sense approach to education – an approach based on discipline and encouragement to those students who did not quite have the educational maturity to achieve at their highest at that time. No students were left behind, but those students were not allowed to disrupt the learning process of those higher achieving students.

Discipline was upheld for the benefit of all teachers, students, and community. Coach was the rock behind that approach. He booked no nonsense. Students achieved at all levels. He was truly blessed in his ability to touch, to reach out, and communicate that he cared about all of the students under his care.

Later in his life he became increasingly concerned with the direction of school business in teaching and how schools were being led. We had many discussions concerning the lack of strong directional leadership based on the forgotten common sense approach to educating young people.

As I became a teacher, coach, and administrator I leaned on Coach for professional advice. Many times I would call him to pull up from his wisdom, and he was always quick to tell me if I was wrong or he thought someone was making a mountain out of a mole hill.

When our oldest son Paul was ready to begin playing football, I asked Coach to speak with him in the privacy of his office without my presence. He of course told me to bring Paul to his office. I did so and turned to walk out when I was instructed to sit. Coach then began to inform Paul to play football because he wanted to and not to play for the S.O.B. as he pointed to me. Paul understood that, and so did I.

During my high school playing days, I remember an event of Coach meting out discipline to one of our best players when he forgot his uniform pants. As an adult and high school coach myself, I told Coach he should have been arrested for breaking school property, and using unusual force and physical discipline in correcting said player. That event happened in Elba, Alabama.

I also gave Coach a hard time for ever thinking he could make an offensive lineman out of me. He chose to play me on the left side of the line never knowing I was deaf in my right ear. I never could get off the snap count, and he would get very frustrated. When I informed him I did not want to play on the offensive line, he asked me very frankly, "When did you become a damn coach?" I understood immediately.

In closing, Coach was a "results man." He was no nonsense when it came to coaching and playing. He did not care about your personal feelings as player. He cared about performance and representation. He challenged you to be proud of who you were and where you came from. As a player, he wanted it to mean something when you put that Wildcat uniform on.

Greg Arrington

My nickname is Possum. Let me tell you how I got that moniker.

To begin with, I was paddled early and often by Thad Morgan, but the most memorable paddling incident did not involve Mr. Morgan as the paddle wielder, famous though he was. Coach Ben Baker had Doug Lee and me in his car before he arrived. I was seated in the back seat. Not unusual for a boy from Clayhatchee, I had a strand of sandspurs from my pants, handed them to Doug in the front seat, and told him to put them in coach's driver's seat. He did.

Coach Baker was not happy with either of us after he reseated himself in the car. After extracting the stickers from his backside, he stopped outside Thad Morgan's office at the old high school, rapping on the window to get Mr. Morgan's attention. He asked to borrow Thad's paddle. When Mr. Morgan heard the explanation, he not only gladly handed the dreaded paddle through the window, he stayed to enjoy the repeated application of it to Doug's bottom and my own. I can still recall his ear-to-ear grin as he watched and listened. That was my introduction to Thad and his paddle.

Fast forward to the last game of the season in 1975. Doug and I were juniors at EHS. We Wildcats were the home team against the Dothan Tigers, quarterbacked by Steadman Shealy before he headed off to play for the Bear. After practice the Thursday before the game, Doug and I, joined by several more players, went to Clayhatchee to catch possums (they may be called opossums in other places, but around here they are possums). The idea we had was they would be released at Bates Stadium during the football game. We were outstanding hunters that evening because we caught six fine possums and put them in a large croker sack. We put a small hole in the sack and left them near my house.

The next day, Friday - game day, while I was in Mrs. Cousins' class, I "suddenly remembered" that I had left my football cleats at home and needed to get them. Mrs. Cousins bought my story and Brad Brackin drove me home where I picked up not my shoes but a croker sack with one lone possum in it. The others had nosed their way out of the sack through the hole. This possum was way too fat to escape. We had one possum left, but he was a fine specimen of possumhood and could probably do the job.

Because we played football we would not be the ones to release the possum. That task fell to Alan Lindsey and Randy Johnson so we left the sack and its contents with them. They lay in wait outside the stadium fence and at an appropriate moment in the game dropped the opened, untied sack over the fence. You would have thought the possum had been trained. We could not have scripted his moves any better. He scurried straight down the middle of the field. Doug swears he was under center when the referees called a possum timeout.

The refs went after the possum that was having no part of their officiating.

Police were called down to the field. They tried shining bright lights into its eyes. Interrogation technique? The possum resisted arrest.

Fox Fleming saved the day. He strode onto the field like a giant, snatched up the possum, and took it over to the sideline to show "Coach" Morgan.

We went on to lose the game to Dothan. Perhaps Fox was not the hero. Could we have mounted a comeback inspired by a Clayhatchee possum? We'll never know.

ADDENDUM: My senior year, as we players were turning in our uniforms at the end of the season – a season in which we beat Dothan in Dothan, Coach Bacon beckoned to me with his little index finger to "come here" (a gesture any teenage boy dreads seeing).

"How did you get the nickname Possum, Greg?" he asked, staring rather intently at me. I looked him straight in the eye and spilled my guts about the whole possum encounter...and I would have spilled them even more quickly if Thad Morgan and his paddle had asked the question.

Kenneth Valrie

I first met Mr. Morgan in 1977. I was coming out of Yancey Parker's Clothing Store after getting fitted for our football banquet at Dauphin Jr. High School. Mr. Morgan looked at me and asked me what my name was. I told him, and then he said, "Hell, I know your name. I am the one who is going to beat your a** if you get into trouble."

He is one of three mentors in my life. He always told me he never wanted to hear nothing but the truth. He set a standard for being not only a Wildcat but for being a better man. He believed that you can achieve any task if you work hard.

Through high school, college, and coaching, I have always tried to adhere to Mr. Morgan's values in trying to be a standup citizen. He was a man who loved, loved whipping your a**, but he was a father to many. I thank him for what he has done for me and my family. May he rest in peace.

Mike McQueen

Saturday Night Fever was burning up the box office while TV sets were turned to Happy Days and Charlie's Angels. My father had loaded my brother and me up into his Chrysler to make the long trip from Virginia to Enterprise so that we could arrive early and get started in our new hometown. This is where we would start our new life, and this is where my life would change.

"Do you play football, boy?"

Those were the first words I ever heard Thad Morgan speak, and they were directed at me as I stood in his office in the summer of 1977. I had played the previous two years at two different high schools – one in Hawaii and one in Virginia – who collectively hadn't won three games total, and they certainly didn't take football as seriously as this town did.

I listened to the gravelly voiced bulldog of a man lay out the expectations of a Wildcat player both on and off the field, not like a school official, but more like a guardian – like a knight Templar of Enterprise Wildcat Football. As I stood in that wood-paneled office with my father, I was fully aware that things were going to be different.

As I started practicing with my new teammates, I noticed that Principal Morgan spent quite a bit of time around the team. He was also frequently carrying a wooden paddle with him, something I was not used to seeing and something he didn't carry just for show!

At first it was a bit unsettling to hear the "pop" and then the howl that followed my friends as they were on the receiving end of that wooden paddle, but I wasn't worried. In order to be punished, I figured you had to break the rules. My mistake! Sometimes rules were broken, but Thad Morgan's rules were far more arbitrary and unique, as determined by a panel of one – him!

My baptism by board came on an August afternoon as I lay on my stomach in the training room, reading an *Athlon* pre-season football preview, waiting to get my ankles taped.

I heard someone walk in the door, but I didn't look up. Next, I heard a "whoosh" as the wooden paddle sliced through the air towards my backside, covered only by a thin pair of gym shorts. Smack! I leaped off the table and stared at Mr. Morgan with incredulity and hollered, "What was that for?!?!"

He grinned at me and said, "Welcome to the Wildcats." Then he turned and walked out the door.

As I grew older, I was able to determine how much of the "gruff" was an act, and how deep Thad Morgan's love would run. I saw an entirely different side of this man when our youngest son Parker became a part of the special education program. Thad had a passion for these unique children that was even more intense than his passion for football.

His concern was for every student, but his driving force was to make sure every child was given every opportunity to become all that they were capable of being. He was truly as proud of the special needs singing group The Heartthrobs as he was of the state championship football team.

If the measure of a man is how he treats those who cannot help him, "the least of these," the same as those who can, then Thad Morgan's life made him a great man indeed. An exceptional man. A man I will never forget.

I'll close with a quote from the movie *Sandlot*:

"Remember kid, there are heroes and there are legends. Heroes get remembered but legends never die..."

Thad Morgan – my mentor, my friend – will always be a legend of epic proportions! He epitomizes the saying, "Once a Wildcat, always a Wildcat!"

Students

Barry Moore

U.S. Congressman from Enterprise, Alabama

Mr. Morgan was truly one of a kind. And even that description seems too cliché. There was no one like him. He had always been an encourager in my young years – boosting me up and making feel like I was important. Then when I thought I had arrived as a young state representative, he sat me down in the Waffle House and gave me "what for." I needed it. He had been good enough to me in my life that I took his tough love in stride and his wise counsel to heart. It will always be with me. And I know his influence in many others.

Jeffrey Smith

In my sophomore year in the mid 1970s at Enterprise High School, during our morning break, I was sitting in the north-eastern most class on the 4th hall waiting for Health Occupation Class (taught by Peggy Waldrop). I was alone in the room reading (imagine that). Principal Thad Morgan walks in to show a classroom to two distinguished Black gentlemen. They appeared to be educators or NAACP officials.

They had just been through the designated smoking area between the 3rd and 4th halls next to the two tennis courts. Thad nodded at me and the two other men smiled.

One of the visitors said to Thad, "I am amazed at the race relationship harmony here. Both races intermingle freely and don't break off into racially segregated groups. How have you achieved this?"

Thad responded, "When they act up, we beat both races with a paddle. It evens out by color."

Ed.'s note. Jeffrey Smith is a graduate of Enterprise High School and is a practicing physician in Upstate South Carolina. He has written three murder-mystery novels and 18 works of non-fiction. One of his books is *A Lingering Evil: The Unsolved Murder of Buford Lolley* about a murder that took place in Enterprise in 1968. Another book he wrote was published by Outskirts Press. The title of that book is *A Pea River Progeny: Alabama's Colorful and Controversial Governor James E. "Big Jim" Folsom*. Folsom was a native of Elba, Alabama.

Susan Judah

Thad Morgan....mentor, friend, principal, father figure, co-worker, employer, kindred spirit, inspirer, disciplinarian ... are many roles Thad Morgan played in many lives. Yet, I think the title he most deserved and what most people called him, was "COACH," and he coached a slew of us through life. "Coach Morgan,"...just the name warms my heart and evokes both happiness and sadness wrapped into one. Happiness, because almost every encounter with him included laughter, and sadness because he has now left us for his heavenly home...well deserved for him, but a void for those left behind.

Initially, I had a bit of fear of Coach Morgan, but once I got to know him, that fear transformed into love, respect, and perhaps even a touch of awe. As an EHS cheerleader, I was part of the crew he always referred to as "troublemakers," a group who got in the way of the all-important sports program.

Believe it or not, coming from Coach Morgan, we considered that a high compliment because it meant he cared enough to recognize us, always calling out to us wherever we saw him or whenever we needed his permission for some activity to cheer on our beloved WILDCATS! And we knew we could absolutely depend on every meeting with him ending with a resounding, "Get the **** out of my office and quit bothering me," which we interpreted (correctly, I'm sure) as, "I really love you girls and am so proud of you!"

It was always a highlight to go to the Principal's office...even if it was to be disciplined. One time... (and I will admit that I was somewhat of a "free spirit" who often had to be reeled in) I got into trouble during exams...for talking of course. I was sent to Coach Morgan's office, and he gave me a choice - three licks or calling my mother. Naturally, I chose the three licks. He gave me three swats and then announced, "NOW you are calling your mother!" In a righteous huff, I called her. He did the talking, and after that I started keeping my mouth shut... most of the time, anyway.

On one particular day in history class, Principal Morgan stopped by to observe our teacher. Immature students that we were, one of our male classmates (whom all the girls liked to impress) referred to the "Elastic Clause," as the "Bra Clause." Another girl and I, wanting to impress, laughed loudly and boisterously. Nothing was said, but during the next class period, the names of the "Bra Clause" boy and the two laughing girls were "asked" over the intercom to come to Coach Morgan's office. By the tone of the announcement, it was clear this was not to be a social call. We were all expecting three licks with the time-honored paddle; instead, Coach Morgan detailed matter-of- fact exactly what we had done wrong.

"I have never been so disappointed in a group of students," he said. "You have embarrassed yourselves, your families, your teacher, and me. I am very disappointed." By that point I was inwardly begging for forgiveness and the three licks, but he simply sent us back to class to wallow in our guilt and repent for our behavior. No paddle has ever hurt as much as disappointing Coach Morgan did that day. I never wanted to let him down again.

For a long time, my dream was to become a teacher in Enterprise City Schools, and after graduating from college, with Alabama education budget cuts deep, I was hired to work at Enterprise High School as a Special Needs Aide. By that time, Coach Morgan was the Superintendent of Education. On the day I went to his office to sign my paperwork, Sammy, my fiancé, drove me over and waited in the car. During my conversation with Coach Morgan, I asked if he wanted to meet my fiancé. "**** NO," he bellowed, "WHY WOULD I WANT TO MEET SOMEONE CRAZY ENOUGH TO MARRY YOU!"

As I was finishing the paperwork, he told me to wait in his office a few minutes. He returned shortly and said he'd see me at teacher institute, to be on time, and not to talk too much. As I left his office, I tried to give him a hug and then returned to Sammy's car. Immediately, a puzzled Sammy told me that some man had come to the car, banged on the window, told him to let the window down, and asked if he was engaged to Susan Provin. Sammy responded that he was, and the man yelled, "Boy, you better run like hell! You don't know what kind of trouble you've gotten yourself into!" Then the man walked away. I just laughed and said, "Oh, Sammy that was Coach Morgan! He loves me!"

The next school year I was very proud to finally get my teaching position at Coppinville Junior High School in Enterprise...a dream come true, BUT that was during a terrible time of proration for Alabama's education budget, and every year new hires were automatically pink-slipped in case funds were not available. For two years, the end of the year brought Coach Morgan to my door with that dreaded pink slip. Although that was a thankless task, he cared enough about his teachers to hand them out personally. Each year I fell apart, grabbed him, and cried. In typical Coach Morgan fashion, he barked, "Get the **** off of me. You are going to be O.K...and quit crying!" I understood then that he was as hurt to give that pink slip as I was to receive it.

At the end of my third year, he was again at my door. I started crying before I even reached the door. "Why, Why, Why" I was asking. This was to be my tenure year." When I opened the door, Coach Morgan was standing there with a flower in his hand and a rare smile instead of his usual scowl. He handed me the flower and announced, "No **** pink slip for you today!"

I jumped for joy, tried to hug him, and he asked, "Why did we hire you in the first place? You are more trouble than you're worth!" The next year I was honored by being named "Teacher of the Year." At the meeting when the awards were presented, Coach Morgan handed mine to me and said, "Who voted for you? They must be crazy!" That was our Coach!

Coach Morgan never approved of Sammy's and my moving to Ozark, and every time he saw Sammy, he'd roar, "Do you know what I like about Ozark....not a damn thing!" On the day I accepted a job in Ozark, I was in the office with Pete Mosley, Superintendent of Ozark City Schools. Dr. Mosley called Superintendent Morgan, and I could hear Coach's voice, loud and clear, rattling off a lengthy list of obscenities. To me it was a love song, and I knew how much he was going to miss me.

This remembrance has been hard for me to write because of the grief I feel. Coach Morgan made such a positive difference in my life, and there is no way to adequately describe what he meant to me. I always thought I was special, but over the years

I have realized that we were all special to him. I was only one of a very blessed crowd. Thad Morgan's manner was unique, off color, rough, and could have easily been misunderstood. But those of us who were fortunate enough to know him and understand him, we are honored to have been paddled, berated, and disciplined, because that was Coach Morgan's true love language.

Susan Provin Judah EHS Class of 1975

John Covington

I was raised in a single parent household by a strong-willed mother who vehemently believed in *Proverbs* "...spare the rod and spoil the child." She perfected the skill of administering vanquishing blows to one's backside and turned, I believe, cussing into an art form. She used both to keep me and my siblings on the straight and narrow.

When I say cussing is an art form, believe me, it is. There is one of tone, diction, appropriate timing, and delivery, and when used in synchronizing harmony there is no doubt whatsoever that the person on the receiving end was more than willing to right any wrong. I didn't know anyone who was better at using the rod or profanity than her, that is, until the fall of 1973.

It was the first day of school. The sound of the bell rang out ending homeroom and ushered students into hallways of Enterprise High School to find their first period class. Then I heard the commanding voice of him walking against the flow of traffic. Now in full view, there he was –Thad Morgan – the man who I would soon learn wrote the book on "cussing" and paddling deserving backsides.

While in the smoking area during break (students were allowed to smoke in school back then in a designated area). I remember quite vividly the warning given to my sophomore friends and me. "Y'all will be alright as long as you don't cross Thad Morgan. Crossing him makes for a very bad day."

I remembered the sound of his voice as he ushered students to first period class hours earlier. It was something in his voice that made me believe everything we were being told about him with my whole heart – just like I believed my mother every time she echoed, "I brought you into this damn world, and I will take you out!"

The days turned into weeks and weeks- months and all were well. I don't recollect exactly when I met Mr. Morgan personally. All I remember is that I was running an errand for Becky Baker, the Distributive Education teacher.

Heard my name, "Johnny Covington."

I turned and walking in my direction was my worst nightmare. Thad Morgan. He never broke stride.

"How are you?"

I responded, "I'm fine."

"Good, how's your momma, and are things going well for her at Enterprise Hospital?"

I told him that she was fine (my mother worked at Enterprise Hospital). I had no clue how he knew my name and where my mother worked.

"Tell her I said hello, and you need to 'git' outta my damn halls and be quick about it!"

I was shaken.

I returned to class with the hall pass and the papers Mrs. Baker asked me to deliver to the office. She asked me where I had been and why I didn't take the papers. I said the very first thing that came to mind..."I forgot," causing the class to burst into a fit of laughter.

With time I became more relaxed whenever I was in Mr. Morgan's presence. Never totally relaxed, however. I have many fond memories of the giant of a man. He was a staunch believer in doing the right thing and for no other reason than it's the right thing to do.

During my senior year I remember him coming to a Student Government Association meeting before Homecoming. He told us that he believed that the Homecoming Court should be representative of the student population and felt strongly that there should be at least two Black senior attendants, and he wanted the SGA's support. When he concluded his remarks as to why he believed it to be important, he was given a resounding applause by the students.

The year ran its course, and it was class ring day, an exciting day for juniors – not so much for me as something had come up and my mother could not afford to purchase my ring. I was disappointed but understood. She always did the very best that she could. My disappointment dissipated by the time I got off the bus at school, and I turned my attention to the speech I was to give for SGA later that morning.

When I finished the speech, Mr. Morgan came down to the edge of the stage and motioned for me. He whispered, "You did a good job. I need to see you in my office after this is over."

"Yes Sir?" I said.

I reported to his office as requested. He handed me one of his personal checks made payable to Balfour, the class ring company and said, "Now go and get that class ring."

No words I can put here would adequately explain how I felt. It had little to do with the ring and more about the man. That was a very happy eye-opening day for me. A few weeks passed, and I asked my mother about repaying Mr. Morgan. She told me that she had taken the money up to the school to pay and personally thank Mr. Morgan, but he refused to take it. That's the kind of man he was.

I could share a story or two about the times he took the paddle to my backside. One time warranted the other times for general principle, but I just don't want to have to recall the pain. Fast forward to Thursday morning June 9, 1994. I was the Principal of the newly constructed Booker T. Washington High School in Tuskegee, Alabama. It was a good day as I was reporting to work happy, relieved, and refreshed. My family had joined me the day before at Auburn University where I received my doctoral degree.

I was drinking my morning cup of Joe in hurried fashion as I had a meeting with the Superintendent of Education at the Central Office. As I was preparing to leave, my Administrative Assistant Mrs. Presley who was a consummate gate keeper, told me that I had a call holding. She knew full well the Superintendent was a lunatic and did not take kindly to tardiness. I told her to take a message and I would call back upon my return to the office. She responded with a very firm voice, "No, you need to take this call now." Her voice and her facial expression were clear.

I let out a sigh of frustration, sat at the desk and answered the call, "John Covington."

Then came the voice on the other end.

"Good morning, Dr. Covington, you old rascal you. I ought to whoop your ass!"

It had been well over a decade since I had heard that voice, but it was one I would never forget.

I said in shock and disbelief, "Mr. Morgan!"

He laughed and he began a rather lengthy diatribe as to how happy he was for me and how proud he was for me. He asked about my mother and requested that I extend to her his very best.

"I know she's proud of you, but I tell you what, she is not one bit prouder of you than I am."

He told me to stay in touch and that he loved me- words that I had never heard from my own father.

Mrs. Presley knew that the conversation had ended by the little light on her phone. She opened the door and found me crying uncontrollably. She closed the door allowing me to have my moment. Now I'm extremely late for the meeting, and I no longer cared. When I got myself together, I couldn't help but laugh as I understood why Mrs. Presley was unable to tell Mr. Morgan that I was unavailable and couldn't put him through. It didn't matter that she didn't know him from Adam. He was Thad Morgan!

Greg Grimsley

Mr. Morgan - he was quite a man. My introduction to him began as a student attending Enterprise High School. I realized quickly as a student that it would not be wise to do anything bad that would get you sent to the principal's office (Mr. Morgan was the Principal) due to the fact that he really could swing a paddle and didn't mind doing it. I heard a lot of stories about that man – even that he had paddled the entire football team!

My high school days were passing, and during this period I would be greeted in the hallways by Mr. Morgan by a firm but sincere "Hey Grimsley." He knew me personally because my mother was the Enterprise City School System Nurse, and one of her bosses was Mr. Thad Morgan.

A couple of years later Mr. Morgan became the Superintendent of the Enterprise City Schools, and I was employed by the system. My mother's office was in the same building as the Superintendent. I worked with quite a unique entourage of educational leaders. These were some of the most honest, trustworthy, hardworking individuals (just good people) for whom I had much respect.

They were Mr. Carter, Mr. Reese, Mr. Tomberlin, Coach Peavy, and Mr. Alford. These men were all led by Mr. Thad Morgan. Daily I watched these individuals work together to better the Enterprise School System. All of these men had the utmost respect for Mr. Morgan. After interacting with Mr. Morgan and the others almost on a daily basis, my conclusion of Thad Morgan was that he loved his family, gave respect and received respect from everyone he dealt with, including my mother and me. My mother had nothing but good things to say about him during her tenure as the school nurse.

Enterprise was very fortunate to have the leaders they had during this era, and the main leader was Mr. Thad Morgan who contributed a lot to the Enterprise School System and the city. It was my honor to know and interact with such a fine man and for him to have such a positive impact on me and many others. I love the City of Enterprise because it was built by many talented and special people like Mr. Thad Morgan.

Ricky Snellgrove

EHS CLASS OF 1972

I was at Old Junior High School when Coach Morgan arrived as a teacher and coach. Just seeing him walk down the halls was intimidating and scary to a young boy with a curious mind. I find it hard to explain that along with commanding presence it was difficult to contain my excitement in the midst of that fear because I KNEW I wanted to be a part of whatever it was he was bringing and that he was going to make a difference in my life. Boy, did he?

I had him for 7th and 8th grade for both basketball and football...heck, I was one of the really lucky ones because I had him for Homeroom too! Our class was the first in Enterprise to see just how tough this man was, and we often joked about how it would be when we moved on to high school and left him for the next "unsuspecting" junior boys even though we knew his name recognition and wild stories would probably reach them long before. Little did we know Coach Morgan was coming with us.

I was BLESSED enough to have his influence in my life from the 7th through 12th grades — most days from sun-up to sun-down. One story that comes to mind is that during our junior high basketball seasons at Old Junior High, he would carry us to junior high games in an old white Biscayne Chevrolet. We were packed in that car like a can of sardines

— sitting sideways and on top of each other. If the car had seatbelts back then, we wouldn't have been able to find one if we tried.

I so remember us going down Highway 27 toward Ozark one night with him driving as if he was going to a fire. We could all sway back and forth banging each other going around those turns and curves exceedingly fast all the while he, at the same time, was talking to us as a collective group and individual "pep talks." Of course, being 7th and 8th graders, we were scared to death not only of his gruff voice and mighty presence, but his driving absolutely brought us closer to the Good Lord as he caused us to greatly increase our prayer lives.

We went on and made memories of a lifetime with this giant of a man. Many years later in one of many conversations with him as Superintendent of the Enterprise City School System, I asked if he remembered those days. His response was, in Coach Morgan's recognizable tone, "Oh Hell yes, I remember them…"

I asked him if he would allow one of his coaches to do that today and he responded, "Why Hell no, Ricky!" with that sheepish grin he always had. Oh, how times have changed over the years! This man was like a second father and mentor to me from the 7th grade to the day he died, and his leadership qualities continue to guide me. He's part of almost daily conversations because that's just how influential he was in my life. I learned under this commanding leadership to never back down to anybody, fight hard in what you believe in, and ALWAYS be damn proud to say you're a

Wildcat! As he said, "Life ain't easy, and it ain't gonna get any easier so y'all better be ready to step up and lead the way!

Coach Morgan. A legend in his own time.

June Crumpler Snellgrove

Coach Thad Morgan...I probably had an advantage of know-ing him even better than most because his family always took precedence in his life; they allowed me to be a part of some-thing special by sharing their family with me. His wife Mrs. Janice had asked me if I would consider being their babysitter for Bitsy and Bill. She knew me as a student, and he knew me as a cheerleader.

It was always an adventure; Bitsy had wit and humor like her dad and knew how to use it to her advantage. She was funny as heck and would sit for an hour at the time brushing my "long red hair" as she described it. To add to this experience, whenever the repetitive motions caused a kink, she would very casually use a few choice words until she got it smoothed out (she knew what she was saying, and I couldn't help but laugh out loud). Bill was a typical little boy who loved mischief and adventure and kept me on my toes.

Whenever it was time for their parents to come back home, we knew there would be a "whoopin" if anyone had misbehaved. Coach Morgan would come in and immediately call out, "Bill, Bitsy, y'all get in here," all the while he was undoing his belt buckle just in case... I always knew I didn't want to be in that line of discipline, but I also recognized that was just his way of say-ing, "Hey kids, I'm home; come in here and let me love on you."

I was blessed to be a Wildcat cheerleader all through junior high and high school years. My daddy and mama never got to see me cheer; I would babysit for money to help pay for my uniforms. After the ballgames I cannot count the times I found myself deliberately walking slowly under the bleachers toward the big, open parking lot just hoping and praying my mama would be there to pick me up. I was scared, and I was embarrassed.

Coach Morgan NEVER allowed me to be alone in "The Hole," and I will love him to the day I die for that assurance. So many times he had Mrs. Janice hang around close enough to protect me and to be on standby to get me home safely – all without making a scene. She did so on many occasions and with such grace. I can still remember the sweetness of her soft and encouraging voice and the distinct sound of the turning signal as we quietly journeyed to my home in the dark of the night. The beauty of this story is that I was just one...only one of many who received this same grace and protection under his leadership.

The gentle giant of Coach Thad Morgan possessed a heart of gold, and he invested his life in making sure every student was accounted for and protected to the very best of his abilities. You'll read and hear from so many how they saw him as a father figure.

I can say to you without hesitation Coach Morgan, whether he was Coach, Principal, or Superintendent, met and exceeded the values and honor that title reflects. He never called me by my first name...only Crumpler; I knew that meant he loved me! That was Thad Morgan. His relationship with students was unlike anything I've ever seen before. I'm just so THANKFUL to have been one fortunate enough be called by my last name...always a Wildcat.

Teri Lee Weeks

A WHOLE FLOCK OF BIRDS

Finally, Thad had finished with business in the school system and business in rebuilding EHS. He could simply walk around the grounds getting his daily exercise, not making life-altering decisions, just choosing which route to take around the school. Inevitably and intentionally, his path always led by the football practice field. On the days when the field was filled with players and coaches, Thad would "shoot them all a bird." He reveled in doing so and laughed about it while I was cutting his hair one day.

I could not help myself. I stepped back from his chair and said, "Next time, do this." Then I spread my arms out and flapped them up and down. He looked puzzled and asked why he would do something like that.

I answered him, "You will be sending them a whole flock of birds!"

His face lit up, and he laughed out loud.

"A whole flock of birds, you say?"

According to coaches and players, Thad did just that – sent them a whole flock of birds every chance he got.

Clare Fleming

(Including A Conversation With Her Father Z.I. Fleming, Jr.)

When Dr. James "Jimbo" Reese called, I was sitting on the back porch "being still." He called to let me know that Thad Morgan's wife had commissioned him to write a book about Mr. Morgan. He wanted to get in touch with my father Z. I. Fleming, Jr. to invite him to share some of his memories of his and Mr. Morgan's times together. They had been educators and colleagues within the Enterprise City School System.

We talked and laughed a bit as he shared a story with me about Mr. Morgan that had been recently recounted to him. I told him that I had grown up hearing stories from my father during those times and that even since returning to Enterprise a couple of years prior, I had heard reminiscent stories on several occasions in which Mr. Morgan was one of the main characters. I gave him my father's cell phone number and told him to let Daddy know that I would help him record his memories. Before hanging up, he invited me to share my thoughts as well.

I believe that we, i.e., the school-aged children who grew up in the Enterprise City School System (ECSS) during the tenure of Thad Morgan as coach, Enterprise High School (EHS) Principal, and ECSS Superintendent, are graced with riches far beyond our capacity to fully understand and the reach of which is immeasurable and eternal. It is the Spirit bestowed upon us and within us Who has then touched and impacted every place and person with whom we have come in contact in that special way that distinguishes us.

I've thought about this often over the past 10 or so years. There was and is a Spirit of pervasive "knowing and receiving" of "good things" that despite our individual failures and humanity (and there were and are inexhaustibly many) over-ruled and "suffered long" and continue to love and embrace us.

I truly believe that Mr. Morgan was called by the Lord to his position. Despite superficial appearances of his being unruly and one who was known for "getting with you," I believe that he must have been drawn by the Lord in a manner that was impossible for him to resist and of which he may not have had full understanding or been fully conscious, especially during those early days. He seemingly just "rolled with the flow" of who he was—not allowing himself to be moved by the opinion of "man."

We who grew up in the ECSS were nurtured, instructed, and taught in the spirit and life of "Do your best." Our teachers, seemingly with "one mind," continually conveyed those expectations to us. They levied them upon us in a "that's-just-how-it-is" manner. We were like freshly plowed land in which seeds were continually being sown and watered and made to thrive despite "stuff" happening.

I believe Mr. Morgan led that charge humbly by just being who he was created to be without pretense or superficiality. The adage, *"The speed of the leader is the speed of the team"* applied here. The fruit that was produced spoke and continues to speak much louder than anything else ever could. We seemingly with ease dominated from within from an innate place in everything from vocational to academics to ROTC to sports to band and *so* much more that came through us from that invisible eternal place.

I personally have come to understand just how blessed we were. In all the places I have been and in everything I have experienced (as a parent, as a former teacher and instructor, as an employee, as a citizen, and much more), not one has come even close to offering the lasting treasures that we received growing up in ECSS located in little Enterprise, Alabama, during the 1970s and 1980s.

> *"Wherefore, by their fruits you shall know them."*
> (Matthew 7:20 KJV)

A Conversation With Z.I. Fleming, Jr. About Thad Morgan

The following is the conversation that my father and I had about Mr. Morgan on July 10, 2023. I was blessed and afforded the opportunity and privilege of hearing new stories and hearing additional details of old stories.

Clarissa "Clar" Fleming
EHS Class of 1985

(Note that for the purpose of authenticity, I attempted to capture and keep his dialect, "voice", and tone intact). Therefore, brackets of additional information are used throughout to aid the reader's understanding. Italics are used to express emphasis and italicized phrases are used to express places within the conversation where there was much laughter.

Clar

When did you and Mr. Morgan meet?

Daddy

Sometime between 1969 and 1971.

I knew of him prior to actually meeting him. I was Coach [Alfred] Peavy's assistant athletics coach [at Coppinville High School (CHS)]. Mr. Morgan was the head coach of all athletics at Enterprise Junior High School (EJHS). I observed during that time he worked hard at "coaching."

Coppinville played Enterprise Junior High at EJHS. Coppinville beat Enterprise Junior in that first game. During that game, they wanted to shoot set shots and Coppinville blocked many of the [EJHS] shots. When they came to CHS, they beat us because Thad had taught them how to move around and shoot jump shots. They were good shooters if they were allowed to set up, but set shots took more time than jump shots.

Clar

If he were still Superintendent of Schools or Principal of Enterprise High School (EHS), how do you think he would handle the civil unrest that we are currently experiencing at all levels of life in America?

Daddy

He would handle it. You know we had some of it when we were there [within Enterprise City Schools] but it wasn't as aggressive as it is now, and people were not as open with it.

Background (about Sam Picket) beginning:

But that was [during] the time when there was a young man named Sam Pickett. He was one of the guys that when he came, Thad sort of took him under his wings [and continued with Sam] until the day he passed away. Sam was here [when Mr. Morgan transitioned] and was one of the [Mr. Morgan's] pallbearers.

Sam was a good football player. And so, he made the football team [and] he became one of the starting defensive ends as a sophomore. Some of the senior boys told him that no sophomore was supposed to play on that line—just only them (the seniors). According to what the guys told me, Sam told them that he "would play where he wanted to play" [even as a sophomore].

So, they went by Sam's place one night and picked up Sam; and they went out somewhere in the woods, and one of them fought Sam. They said that Sam just beat that senior down! The boys "couldn't wait" until the next morning to run and tell me about it. (*Lots of laughter and chuckling as he retold this part*).

When the senior got to my class, the other boys brought up the subject of the fight during our conversation. The player who had been beaten up said, "Mr. Fleming, he [Sam] can play wherever he wants to play." *(More laughter)*

Thad had told me earlier that he had sort of named some of his pallbearers. He said that some of the boys would be telling him, "Coach, you're mean." He told them, "That's all right. "When I'm gone, you're going to be one of the pallbearers."

And... They were... [Yes,] and they were.

Background (about Sam Picket) ending

Many times, we had those [types of] problems. Like for example the "Sam" versus a black student thing."

Clar

So, this is another fight that Sam [Mr. Morgan's boy] had other than with the senior football defensive lineman? What's the background for this fight?

Daddy

Thad handled it. I believe this happened the year before Coach Peavy came when Thad was Assistant Principal [and Mr. Howell was Principal at the high school]. As assistant, he had a good relationship with all the kids—black and white. When we integrated the schools, Thad would come into the black community; he would go to some of the black churches like Friendship [Missionary Baptist Church]—where we had a lot of black kids—and Johns Chapel and talk to parents and students.)

Mr. Howell was sometimes reluctant to enforce some of the good rules that we had. Mr. Morgan would deal with them fairly; but, when it really got solidified is when Coach Peavy transferred over [from Coppinville], I think the next year. When Coach came over there, they had some order—not only with their race, but with both races.)

[Background:] One black student would come down to the [front] office where Sam was a student assistant. He came to the office every day—I'll use the term— "picking at" Sam. Sam was the office assistant and was where he was supposed to have been. I know this because I would visit the administrators in the front office when I started thinking about going into administration. The black student ought to have been in class somewhere but challenged Sam to go to the field house.

It was no secret that Sam would fight, and Sam knew how to fight. He had been reared in a home most of his life that allowed him to be around blacks quite a bit. Because Sam was bigger—he wasn't fat—Boy, . . . I mean he was. . . He was just a good-looking boy. I was told that he was [as] strong as a bull. They went down to the field house, and the black student locked the door. *(Daddy chuckles here at the memory in a way that makes me laugh out loud as well as he's relishing the re-telling of the story.)*

But, in the community Mr. Garth [is] mad, Coach [is] mad, all of them [are] mad [prior to knowing the background]:

[They were saying] "Lettin' them big ol' white boys jump on them little ol' black boys. . ."

So, I said, "Y'all need to know what's going on. Sam was in the right place. And they had told the black student to stay from down there and he should have been in class. But every day he'd be down there 'picking at' Sam.

That would have been like me going down there against Coach Peavy. Now if Coach is fighting hard and I'm fighting hard, I'm going to get beat because he is so much bigger than me. And so, I told them it's the same thing with the black student.

I said "We got to be fair too. When we are wrong or misinformed, we are just wrong or misinformed."

Clar

So . . . you have spoken quite often over the years about these two stories involving you and Mr. Morgan:

1. When you and Mr. Morgan "got into it" and

2. When you and Mr. Morgan often drove to Birmingham to see Coach Peavy when he was in the hospital in Birmingham.

Daddy

Okay, we got into it.

[Background:] The year before I left the high school [1982-1983 school year], we had been talking about me becoming Principal at Coppinville Junior High School.

(I really wanted to stay in math.) That year, we had to assign all teachers in their professionally certified area.

One of the assistant principals who handled the math department identified that we needed to dismiss a teacher who was teaching math because there was another teacher who was *endorsed* to teach English, but who was certified in mathematics and had been at EHS longer. Therefore, she had to leave the English department and go to the math department. (She had been teaching in the English department because she was the sponsor of the Debate Team.)

In the meantime, the teacher that they had to lay off wanted to know why she was being laid off. The assistant principal told her it was "because she wasn't a good teacher." That really bothered that teacher because she truly *was* a *good* teacher. She could teach anything from general math to calculus with ease.

She came to me, Mrs. Rhodes, and Mrs. Taylor [because] we were the senior folks in the math department. I was chairman of the math department at that time so we sat down and talked about it.

I told her, I said, "You know, . . . go talk to Mr. Morgan, he'll tell you why." I don't see why the assistant principal couldn't tell you the truth. It's because you don't have tenure. You're the last one hired and that's the way the system works.

Clar

[Seeking clarification:] Tell her [the truth] that [above background] was the real reason rather than tearing her down?

Daddy

[Tell her] that was the reason, yes.

In the meantime, her husband and Mr. Morgan got into a verbal altercation during the weekend. He called Mr. Morgan, and then on Monday morning, Thad sent for me. Well, he told David Carter to tell me during my planning period to come over because he wanted to talk to me. So, I went in to his office and as soon as I walked in, he said to me,

"I thought [You think] I was [you are] a damn schoolhouse lawyer, didn't I [don't you]?"

And then, I flew back on him and asked him, "What the hell [are] you talking about?" (You know, one of the things [about Mr. Morgan that] he would do is try to dominate the conversation.)

Then I said, "You know, it's bad if we can't, in this school system, send folks to talk to our superintendent when they got problems."

By that time, . . . I mean. . . you know. . . we had said some other things to each other.

And I said, "You got to stop acting the fool like you did on that football field. You are the Superintendent [of Enterprise City School System]."

Clar

What were some of the other things that you all said [to each other]?

Daddy

I don't remember because both of us had gotten mad with each other, and I knew he was trying to convince me to go to Coppinville which [a part of me] did want to go because Mr. Garth had always said, "I want some of you all to be ready to follow me in."

In the meantime, when I fired off on him about *"If we can't send folks to you, then who can we send them to?"* he stopped just like a soldier doing an "about-face." By then, both of us had teared up because we were *[so]* fired up at each other.

Then he said, "Huh? Is that what happened?".

I said, "You need to start listening before you open your mouth. You're the Superintendent. You need to be able to let folks communicate with you. In this school system any principal that I've had (and that's including you), you know I've been supportive of whatever programs we had. If it was something that I didn't think was good, I always went to whoever I should and talked about it."

And then he started, "Z, I'm *so* sorry . . ." but now, I'm mad with him, so I didn't act like I was accepting that apology.

I finally told him, "I got a class, I've gotta go."

So, I got up and left. And then. . . I don't know when he told Coach [Peavy], but he probably went right over [to talk to him] then.

Coach said, "Well Thad, you did the boy wrong. Give him time."

At that time it was getting down to the point where he was trying to select a principal for Coppinville. He often told me that he wanted a principal who was going to be able to make decisions, and he [Mr. Morgan] didn't have to [in reality] be the principal over there. That was his confidence in me. We had both been at the high school together. In fact, he was principal at the high school for five years before he went to the superintendent's office.

Thad wasn't as "bad acting" as folks thought he was. He would tear up in a minute about things that were going on. After he and I had that confrontation, we never did "get into it" again.

Clar

Okay, so the next story I remember is about when Coach Peavy was sick during the time when all of you were still at the high school prior to Mr. Morgan becoming superintendent.

Give us the background for the story about Coach Peavy being sick and you and Mr. Morgan riding up to Birmingham to see him when he was in the hospital.

Daddy

[Background:] Coach Peavy had heart problems. Janice Morgan's brother was a doctor up there at the Methodist Hospital, I think. Anyway, Peavy had many things wrong with him. So, he admitted himself into the hospital. When he was supposed to go up there, Voncille [Coach Peavy's wife] and I tried our best to get him to let me drive him up there. Mr. Garth tried to get him to let somebody drive him, but he wouldn't let any of us drive him. When Coach got to the hospital that first time, he said he was *so* sick.

Somewhere between Montgomery and Birmingham at a service station sitting on a hill, Peavy said he had stopped there and had to literally get on his knees and crawl to get back into his automobile, but he drove on up to Birmingham. He said that he didn't know [how]—but I guess it was the providence of the Lord—[that] he drove onto the ramp that took him right up to the nurse's station. He said when he got there, they somehow noticed he wasn't moving very well. They told him he had the highest blood pressure of anybody who had ever been at that hospital up to that point in time.

We had the inside track for checking on him because Thad would call his brother-in-law and tell him, "Tell me what's going on! Go find out!"

Thad and I would drive up to see him. They would *always* let *me* in. But then, at first, they wouldn't let Thad in.

On this particular time, they said, "Well, only family. . ."

Thad said, "Hell, I'm family too! That's my brother." *(Daddy chuckles at the memory.)*

After that they would let him in. Also, [because] Thad was pretty well-known all over Alabama, once they heard his name, they [were willing to] let him in [to see Coach Peavy].

Clar

Okay. All right. . . Do you have anything else you want to say about Mr. Morgan?

Daddy

Like I said, Thad was always fair to me. [The one time] when he wasn't, he didn't hold it against me when I retorted on him. Even when Colleen [Gordon] went to the [superintendent's] office, I know he supported her when some of the personnel in the office were [talking behind her back] saying [for example] that she "dressed too good." At first, she would go crying to Thad. He told her that she knew he had told them not to do it, but that he couldn't just sit there and monitor it.

He told her, "Do what you have to do, and I am going to

support you. If you don't think I will support you, go to Z and ask him what I did when. . ."

[Background:] A parent [who sometimes substituted as a nurse in the school system] was insubordinate toward me [when he was principal at Coppinville Junior High School] and called the police when I requested that she correct a matter that had been brought to my attention. [Later when he had gone to the Superintendent's office] When a colleague who worked in the Superintendent's office "counseled" me not to "get myself in trouble," Thad overheard some of the conversation and asked me what it was about. After I told him, Thad said, "Hell, I don't have but one principal at Coppinville."

He directed the colleague to come to Coppinville and apologize. That colleague and I talked about it for a good long while and continued to have a good working relationship after that incident.

When she [Colleen] came to me, I [also] told her to "Cuss their butts out! You don't have to take that mess. Cuss their butts out!" So, you know, she finally got where she would. . .

(Clar, laughing out loud, interjects question, "Cuss their butts out?")

Daddy: "Yeah. . . cuss their butts out!" *(Daddy is laughing as he adopts his two-octave lower voice that he would use during such occasions and "puts on" his no-nonsense face that he displayed during that conversation—I guess, to show Mrs. Gordon how to do it.)*

(Clar, who is by this time "rolling on the floor" laughing says,

"Okay. . .Oh, goodness!")

Clar

So, Daddy, what are your final words regarding Mr. Morgan?

Daddy

I believe Mr. Morgan was an *exceptionally* great educator and administrator in all the roles [in which] he served—as coach, as assistant principal, and as superintendent. I *deeply* respected him as a person.

Teachers and Other Employees

Judi Lee Stinnett

EHS class of 1966 and EHS teacher 1982-1998
PAIN

Pain is a word many an Enterprise High School graduate associates with Mr. Thad Morgan, former coach, principal of EHS, and Enterprise superintendent of education. One does not have to have been an athlete or even a male to be blessed by the pain Thad could inflict with his ever-present paddle, although a high percentage would fit into both categories. If a large number of the tales of this book do not revolve around paddlings applied to the posteriors of the authors of the tales, I will be shocked. I just hope each one includes the obligatory "thank you" Thad required after each application.

Unlike so many others, story about pain inflicted by Thad does not involve his paddle though. It is tied to my earliest memory of Thad Morgan. My brother and Thad were friends, two of a large group of guys who liked to hang out together. Ten years younger than they, I was brazen enough to toddle along after them and get in the midst of their gatherings.

On this particular day, one of the guys had driven his motor scooter over to our house, and maybe six or eight were clustered around it on our postage-front yard. I had heard the scooter as it putt-putted in and rushed outside as fast as my five-year-old legs could carry me. Feeling as if I were in a forest amidst all those guys, I started jerking on the nearest pants leg I could reach, begging to be put on the scooter. Thad was the one whose pants leg I yanked, and he swung me onto the scooter. Not Bad. Good Thad – right?

Wrong! The scooter had been driven either a long distance or a long time, and the exhaust pipe was extremely hot. I yowled. And I remember nothing after that happened.

I bear the scar on the back of my right calf to this day. And I have always remembered who put me on the scooter. Good Thad put me up there. Bad Thad burned my leg. All of my other associations with Thad Morgan after that were with Good Thad.

FIRED OR HIRED?

Repartee. I am not sure Thad Morgan would have ever used that word. He would have preferred "snappy comeback" or "wisecrack." He would have said such a person was being a wise***. He would certainly know because he himself was a master of —-repartee. He also appreciated anyone who gave him a sharp comeback. In fact, he savored a quick retort.

But I knew none of those traits when I was sent to him for what I thought was the rest of my job interview. It was the summer of 1982. My mother had been diagnosed with cancer, and we were looking for an opportunity to move closer to Enterprise to be able to care for her. I had applied for the rare English opening at Enterprise High School and had interviewed with David Carter and an assistant principal as well. They then sent me to Thad Morgan. I probably had not talked to Thad Morgan since he set me on a motor scooter that burned my leg, but I certainly knew the growing legend of Thad. I wondered what kind of interview I would have.

I was barked into his office and ordered to sit. He jabbed a finger toward a ratty looking, low-sitting couch, but I eased farther into his office and took a chair on the far side of his desk. He sat very still for what seemed an interminable period of time just frowning at me.

"Who told you not to sit on that couch?" he growled.

I, too, sat for a period of time, searching my mind for an appropriate answer. "Why would anyone sit on that thing?" issued from my mouth without my permission.

Another eon passed as his eyes bored into mine. I grew smaller, I am certain, as I wished to disappear. But I did not drop my eyes. I matched his stare.

"Well, do you want this d*** job or not?" he asked. Consternation must have showed on my face or maybe it was simply confusion, because I blurted, "I am here for an interview."

D*** the interview! Do you want the job?"

Another silence. I did, then, look down at my clenched hands in my lap.

"Since you make it so attractive, I don't see how I can refuse." Again, those words came out of my mouth without my paralyzed brain's permission.

I jutted my chin in his direction.

His shouted diatribe which followed paralyzed the rest of my body.

"I want you to understand I am not hiring your brother Bo. I am not hiring your mother, and I am not hiring your daddy. I am hiring you're a**. And if you don't do the kind of job I expect you to do, I am not going to fire your mother or your daddy. I am going to fire your a**. Now, do you want the job or not?" Yes or no!"

Ice cream brain freeze is nothing compared to the painful ruminations that boiled through my head. I thought of my mother. I thought of what Thad said. I thought of moving to Enterprise and taking a pay cut. I thought of turning down the job offer. I thought of how much I wanted to teach at EHS.

I said, "Yes," then stood and held out my hand across the corner of his desk. I continued, "I'll do the best job I know how to do to turn out students you will be proud of."

He stood up, shook my proffered hand, smiled, and said "Deal."

Strangest interview I ever had!.

Dan and Pat Presley

Thad Morgan was a man who showed his love for the Enterprise School System every day of his life.

I (Pat) had the privilege of working under Mr. Morgan as a third grade teacher for 42 years. He was a stable man, and you always knew where he stood. During my teaching career, after working under three superintendents, I can truly say Mr. Morgan impressed me the most.

Our entire family loved and respected him as a family man and as a superintendent. Both of our boys, Phillip and Stephen, attended the Enterprise School System for 12 years, and to this day they still tell stories about Mr. Morgan – some sad, some strict, some funny, some good – but always with respect. He left many happy memories with us that we will always cherish.

Dave Sutton

Thank you for allowing me to be a part of a review of a Great Man's past life. It was a great pleasure not only to know Thad Morgan but to have worked with a true professional.

In regard to my many experiences with Mr. Morgan, I will give you the best quote I can remember. It comes from the interview for the position to lead the Senior ROTC program at Enterprise High School.

I knocked on his office door and was told to enter. With that deep sounding voice he told me to be seated.

"Sutton, do you know what the Yellow Star that the Cadets wear on their uniforms means? Let me tell you that means Honor Unit With Distinction, and if you lose that you will be fired. Now get out and go to work. You are hired!"

For the next several years I served in that position until I ran and was elected Sheriff of Coffee County, serving for the next 16 years.

John Baker

#1 Mr. Morgan My High School Principal and My Boss

When our family moved from Washington D.C. to Enterprise in the summer of 1975, I was about to start my junior year at EHS. Mr. Morgan was the Principal of Enterprise High School at the time. I had no idea the impact he would have on my life.

However, in 1975 as a high school student, my biggest challenge was getting to class on time. After several tardies I was summoned to Mr. Morgan's office. He asked why I couldn't get to class on time. I gave him some lame excuse about I couldn't get my locker open when actually I was probably just socializing. Mr. Morgan was not very impressed with my answer. He asked me to put my hands on his desk and bend over. At that exact moment he asked, "Hey...aren't you the new boy?" Before I could say yes I heard (and felt) the first WHACK!!!!!! There were two or three more to follow, but my memory fails me...or it could have been the pain that made me forgetful. "Lessons learned in blood are not easily forgotten!!!"

Fast forward to the summer of 1985. Kim and I were teaching in Americus, Georgia. We had just returned from a European Concert tour with the Americus High School Singers. On a side note the connection between Americus and Enterprise was very strong. My principal at Americus High School was Richard Fussell. Mr. Fussell was originally from Opp and was a roommate of Mr. Morgan at Auburn.

The Superintendent of the Americus City Schools was Spencer Davis who married an Enterprise girl. Mr. Morgan was also an acquaintance of Alton Schell, the legendary Head Football Coach at Americus High School. Years later I learned that Hinton Johns was a coach during some of the great years at Americus HS.

Back to my story...after we returned from the European tour, I learned that Randy Holmes, my high school choir director, was leaving Enterprise High School to become the choir director at Austin High School in Decatur, Alabama. Randy contacted me as well as did Mr. Morgan about the open position. I asked Mr. Morgan if I could discuss it with Kim before I made a decision.

He said, "Do you want this job or not?"

I took the job with Kim's blessing.

During the course of the interview Mr. Morgan reminded me of the paddlings he gave me during my time as a student.

He said, "I beat your ass as a student, and I'll do it again if you get out of line!!!"

Back to the connection between Americus and Enterprise. During my interview with Mr. Morgan I discovered he not only knew Richard Russell but also knew the superintendent and coaches as well as their nicknames: Spencer Davis aka "Onion" Davis" and Coach Alton Schell aka "Knot" Schell.

I'm sure Mr. Morgan had an aka...I never found out what it was.

#2. *YOU CAN HAVE IT WHEN...*

One of my first meetings with Mr. Morgan after being hired as the Choral Director at Enterprise High School, Dauphin and Old Junior was asking for money for choir risers, sound equipment and music. I was very well prepared. I had written quotes from the different companies I wanted to work with as well as why we needed the items.

I felt like I presented my case well and how it was essential to the growth of the program. Mr. Morgan reviewed the proposal quietly and seriously and then looked up and said..."You can have all of this stuff when you find a dog that can s**t money."

Obviously I didn't get any of the items I asked for at that time. However, several years later after the choir program grew and became successful, we got everything we needed and more.

The joke around the school for years was that Baker finally found that dog!!!

Jamie Baker

Thad Morgan The Biggest Disguised Heart

In 1989 I graduated from Auburn University with a Masters of Education Degree in Vocal Music Education and was applying for a teaching job in various areas around and in the state of Alabama. Having married my first soul mate Wendy Lynn Aycock in 1986 while we were both juniors in college, it was imperative to find a job that would support the two of us.

In July of 1986 I had an interview with the Superintendent of Education of the Enterprise City School System Mr. Thad Morgan for the Junior High School Choral Music position. This involved all three junior high schools. I remember Wendy and me driving to Enterprise and wondering what we were doing interviewing in an area of the state that we knew nothing about.

After meeting with Mr. Z.I. Fleming, Jr, at Coppinville, Mr. Perry Vickers at Dauphin, and Mr. Bob Tomberlin at Enterprise Junior, I had the privilege of interviewing with Mr. Morgan. Needless to say, I was not prepared for that interview and if I could add, I never would I have been prepared for it.

As I walked into his office, I was greeted by this gruff sounding man who peered at me above his glasses and asked me to sit down on his sofa. The significance of this particular sofa was that it was so much lower than his desk that it appeared that he was on his throne looking down upon you. Let me say, it worked! It was quite intimidating. You knew exactly who was in charge of everything in the Enterprise City School System.

During the interview process the one thing that stood out to me was the love, compassion and dedication Mr. Morgan had for the Enterprise City School System and for its students and teachers. We all know that he could and did use some colorful language when addressing you and certain topics concerning school.

I learned quickly that if he didn't like you, he wouldn't "cut up" with you in that manner. His love, compassion and dedication were demonstrated toward me in my four years under his leadership. He always had my back as a teacher and supported almost everything I did and presented to him. There were times that I remember him telling me, "HELL NO! YOU AIN'T GETTING THAT," or "HELL NO! YOU DON'T NEED THAT!" I realized all of that came with the territory.

He will always be remembered as a FOREVER WILDCAT who supported and loved his students and teachers and who had a heart so big that it was sometimes hard to see due to the gruffness of his personality.

Martha Thompson

To know Thad Morgan was to love him! Through the years anytime his name was mentioned, admiration and respect were anticipated and heeded. He always seemed so "gruff," but his heart was made of gold. If there was anything he could do to help someone, he was already helping before he was asked. There will never be another like him with his love for our Enterprise School System!

Before being interviewed and hired by him, I was intimidated because of the stories I had heard about his blunt mannerisms. After the interview, I left with a new respect for our school system. He told me that he was only "concerned for what was best for the student, and he would back me as a teacher as long as I remembered that." After my years of teaching, those words of his are still so true and describe him perfectly in regard to his tenure with the Enterprise City School System!

Danny Meeks

It was 9:15 and Symphonic Band class was about to arrive when I got a call from the Boss.

"Get over to my office right now!"

I tried to explain that I had a class coming in, but he would have none of it.

"Get somebody to sit with them. I want to see you now!"

All the way to Mr. Morgan's office I was trying to think of anything I might have done that was out of line. I mean he had already fired me six times since he hired me. I couldn't come up with anything so I walked into his office and proceeded to take my usual place on the sofa in front of his desk, the one that put you about a foot lower than eye level.

"No. Sit in that chair," referring to the nice wooden chair across from the desk. I'm thinking I must have done something he approved because my office status had improved immeasurably.

"Pull it around by me," he said.

I complied.

Mr. Morgan then proceeded to ask how things were going, how the family was doing, and just general chit-chat, all the while taking out an unopened pouch of Bull of the Woods chewing tobacco. He cut off a quarter of the whole plug, stuck it in his jaw and handed me the tobacco pack and his knife. He then placed a trash can between his chair and mine. Now I'm getting it; it's a test. So I cut off another plug and stuck it in my jaw. I chewed myself on occasion.

The conversation continued. After a couple of minutes he leaned over and spit his juice into the can. I was close behind him as that was the worst tasting stuff I had ever chewed. More conversation. All the while I'm starting to get a lot of tobacco juice build up and could hold it no longer, or so I thought . I leaned over to spit into the can and I heard, "Uh Uh Uh! Ain't your turn!"

"What?"

"Ain't your turn!"

As I was holding the juice and turning what I know was a putrid color of green, Mr. Morgan let me sit a while longer with this wry smile on his face. I think I might have bumped his head as I was right behind him getting that awful stuff out of my mouth.

There are multiple stories I could tell you, but this one makes me laugh. During my 25 years of teaching the Enterprise City School System, I could never imagine working for anyone else. Mr. Morgan was never a Superintendent who stood behind his teachers – he stood in front of them. I am forever grateful he recommended me in July of 1979 (that's another study) and put into motion a great place for Mary and me to build out family. With all my heart I thank you, Mr. Morgan.

Charlie Ford

My first memory of Mr. Morgan was my sophomore year in high school with him standing in the hall in the morning with a paddle either in his hand or in his back pocket. He never paddled me, but I was always a little scared of him from stories from friends of mine whom he did paddle.

My next real memory was when I went into his office to be offered the job as Band Director of Enterprise Junior High School (Old Junior). I was with Bill Hickman, the EHS Director along with Bob Tomberlin, EJHS Principal. I had to sit on (more in than on) that couch with no legs that everyone who ever went into there was familiar with. Mr. Morgan did not even look at me. He proceeded to tell Mr. Hickman and Mr. Tomberlin how he wished he could get better people for their jobs. I wish I could remember the conversation, but at that point I was a little concerned that we were all going to be thrown out of the office and I would be without a job. After their berating, he just looked at me and said, "You want the job?"

I said, "Yes Sir."

He then asked if these two had explained to me what would happen if I couldn't keep my hands off the girls or the money. He worded that a little differently. LOL. I told him they did. He had me sign an official offer, and THEN threw us all out of his office. It was quite an experience for sure!

After the tornado of March 1, 2007 high school students and teachers were relocated to Enterprise State Junior College. During our tenure there, I had an incident that many will remember. I asked one of my students to move my truck from the parking lot into the loading dock area so I could unload several tubas that I had picked up from getting repairs. The student decided to give another student a driving lesson with my truck. The result was that the trainee ran the truck INTO one of the portable classrooms we had set up for classes. It was not my best day.

The following day I had to meet with the architects about our new band room facility. In attendance were several administrators including our Superintendent of Education Dr. Reese as well as Mr. Morgan who was assisting the architects. Of course EVERYONE in the room had heard about the previous day's "incident" so when I walked in I was again afraid that I might be without a job soon.

Mr. Morgan looked at me with total disdain and then proceeded to laugh out loud at me. It was definitely deserved. It also helped to ease my nerves just a little before the meeting. Dr. Reese probably remembers inviting me into his office for a private "butt whipping" after the meeting, which I also deserved. Let me add that Dr. Reese, although matter of fact, was extremely polite to me and left me feeling much better. I did NOT let students drive my vehicle again.

This may be my favorite memory of Mr. Morgan. We were taking the band to a large parade in San Antonio in the spring of 2014. While rehearsing one afternoon outside on the street that basically surrounds the current EHS facility, Mr. Morgan was walking by. He used to walk out there often.

I was berating the band about something at that moment, and just as he got to the front of the band and I was finishing my "intense instruction," out of his mouth came these words: "They would probably be better if they had a band director worth a damn!" Remember this was many years after he had retired, and none of the kids knew who he was. In my present state, I am sure the kids were all expecting me to blow up on him. Instead, all I said was, "Yes Sir! You are probably right!"

He did not break his pace, and we went on with our rehearsal. I had SEVERAL kids come to me after rehearsal asking, "Who was that man?" and "Why did you let him talk to you that way?" I had no explanation they would have understood. You just can't make this stuff up.

My last story is pretty short and simple. After moving into the new school, Mr. Morgan along with several of the former administrators, as well as many of the present ones, would watch the football games in the press box. One night after a particular good half time performance, he hollered at me as I was coming out of the announcers' box to tell me how good we did that night. Although we all know Mr. Morgan loved all things EHS, getting a compliment from him was rare, and that one comment from him made my night, and I will always remember it. He really was a great man!!!

Gloria Abernathy

STORY #1

When Thad Abernathy was three weeks and three days old, we moved to Enterprise with a baby boy named after Thad Morgan!!! Mr. Morgan came to the Abernathy's house to see the baby and to welcome us to Enterprise.

STORY #2

Charlie told me that he was meeting Mr. Morgan at his house on Cherry Hill Road. Charlie said Mr. Morgan was "giving Janice hell" for not having things packed already for a "road trip" football game. According to Charlie Mr. Morgan was "fussin n' cussin..." ready to ride!!"

All the men loaded into the vehicle and sped away. Just outside of town Mr. Morgan told the driver to pull over. Charlie was near enough to hear Mr. Morgan telling Janice over the phone and telling her how sorry he was that he was so "loud, rude, and abusive." When Charlie told me this story, I almost cried. He truly loved and adored his precious Janice.

STORY #3

When Thad Abernathy was three years old, he stood up beside my mother in the stands at Bates Memorial Stadium and said, "Ma-Ma, you see that big man down there? "THAT BIG THAD! I LITTLE THAD!"

Story #4

When Thad Abernathy was three years old, he was hyper and excited in those tall, steep, concrete bleachers at Bates. I struggled to keep him beside me. As young Thad was jumping up each step with sheer enjoyment, I'm telling him, "Thad!!! Come here!!!

Mr. Morgan came down the steps, stopped at my Thad, and said, "Give her hell, Thad! Give her hell! Then he laughed at himself all the way down those steps.

Story #5

While I was teaching kindergarten, I asked Mr. Morgan to come and read a book to my children. Janice chose his and Bitsy's favorite – "I Can Lick 50 Tigers!" Mr. Morgan was so funny and made the kids laugh.

Story #6

When son Gabe was four years old, Mr. Morgan invited Charlie, Thad and Gabe to a "dove shoot." Across the field was parked a very large, very expensive, combine tractor or SOME kind of equipment. Gabe, using Charlie's childhood 410 gun, became suddenly excited, jumpy and hyper and SHOT OUT the window of the farm equipment!!!

Charlie yelled, "Damn, Gabe!"

Mr. Morgan quickly pointed that "famous finger" at Charlie, said, "Don't you say a damn thing to him!!! I'll pay for it, damn it!!"

STORY #7

During the first week of a certain school year Mr. Morgan walked into Harrand Creek Elementary School, hugged me and was about to hurry away when I proudly told him, "I'm starting my 25th year" (so tickled, so happy).

He quickly quipped, "You're just a damn rookie!!"

Oh, how I loved that man!

STORY #8

While teaching at Harrand Creek I had an unfortunate encounter with someone. Choking backing tears and as I explained the situation to Mr. Morgan, he said, "Let me make this as CLEAR as a GOAT'S ass going up a hill...Enterprise City School System does not operate that way!"

Mrs. Colleen Gordon, laughing hysterically, replied, "Very good, Mr. Morgan! Real classy."

Mr. Morgan stuck out that finger and shaking it furiously said, "AND don't you take no sh** off NOBODY!"

When Thad Abernathy went to Heaven, Thad and Janice came to my house. He cried like a baby – all the while telling me, "Now look...you gotta live!"

OOOh how I adored that man!

Rhonda Krafft

Mr. Morgan became Superintendent my first year of high school so I missed out on him as my principal. I had heard many notorious stories about him and admired his love for our school system.

Several years passed after my completion of high school when I received my teaching degree. Of course I wanted to work for Enterprise City Schools with Mr. Morgan at the helm. I applied and was hired at an elementary school. What I soon discovered was that I would have to meet with Mr. Morgan and my principal to get approved. Needless to say, I was very nervous. Mr. Morgan could be very intimidating to say the least. Once we had reviewed everything, Mr. Morgan looked at me and said, "You mean to tell me you want to work for this (expletive)?" I eagerly responded, "Yes, sir!" then quickly looked at my principal with wide eyes! I couldn't believe I had responded that way! Luckily for me, my principal just chuckled and shook his head. I had the job!

One Field Day the entire school was outside enjoying the activities when a jeep stopped by the field, and I heard a gruff voice yell at me, "Hey, what's going on out here?" I would recognize that voice anywhere! Mr. Morgan kept up with all the goings-on with ECS even after his retirement. I measure that memory because that was the last conversation I had with Mr. Morgan. I'm glad he stopped to talk with me!

Mr. Morgan could come across as gruff, but he had a heart of gold...especially for children with special needs. It warmed my heart each time I was lucky enough to be witness to his interaction with these children. Mr. Morgan will be missed by anyone who was fortunate enough to have known him.

Ed.'s Note: Ms. Krafft is one of best kindergarten teachers I have ever seen.

Wanda Motes Gardner

When Fob James was Governor of Alabama, Mr. Thad Morgan made it his business to stay on top of what was going on with the state and the Alabama Board of Education. At this time Governor James had the State Department of Education form a committee that would develop a standardized evaluation instrument so that every teacher in the state could be evaluated using its instrument. The committee worked and worked and came up with this instrument.

I don't personally know what all was on the instrument but knew there were about 30 things that the administration was supposed to look for when observing the teachers. It was designed so that there was no writing for the observers, just areas to bubble in. If the teacher did the listed activity, he/she got a bubble. If the teachers were very good, there were lots of bubbles on the page at the end of the observation.

When the committee got ready to pilot the instrument, Thad already knew all about it. He proceeded to volunteer EHS to be a pilot school. I don't remember how or where Thad first told me about it, but at some point, he did tell me that they would be coming to my classroom to observe. I felt like they would observe one of my regular math classes, but four people walked into my highest level Fifth Year Math Class.

This class was the first classroom that had a computer in it to be used for instruction at Enterprise High School. This was before software so students were programming the computer to do math. At most, there could be two students programming at a time. I was teaching whatever the lesson was to the rest of the class that included two Italian students, one Norwegian and a German student. English was a second language for all four of them.

That day I ran my class like every other day as if the observers were not even there. I taught the lesson in English and wrote the lesson and examples on the board. Then I would go to the students for further instruction individually. I had at least a little background in Italian so we could communicate a little. I could only communicate in numbers with the students from the other two countries, but we did what we could, and I moved on to help all the rest of my students with the lesson. I would then go and check on the students programming.

The observers didn't have bubbles for all that! They were very complimentary, but the instrument was not adequate for what they were seeing. They reported what they found back to Thad. The instrument was not seen back at EHS!

This story has nothing to do with me. It speaks to Mr. Morgan staying on top of education in Alabama. Seeing the futility of the instrument and doing what he could to stop it just showed that Mr. Thad Morgan knew his teachers, he knew education, and he understood politics and how to take care of business!

Thad and Punctuality

To appreciate this you have to know that David Carter, then Principal of Enterprise High School, was extremely punctual.

He would be the first to arrive at any event – one of those "if you show up on time, you are late" kind of people.

This particular morning in 1984 Mr. Carter and I were to meet Mr. Morgan in front of his office at 7:30 to drive to Montgomery to represent EHS as it was being recognized by the Department of Education for being in the top 100 schools in the nation and for my winning the Presidential Award for Excellence in Mathematics.

So 7:30 comes and goes and no Thad. Mr. Carter, getting antsy, was going over the plan for getting to Montgomery with me. He would be driving the three of us which told me that there would be no stops. It was probably a quarter to 8:00 before Mr. Morgan meandered out. I knew as soon I looked at him that he was up to something. He would get a little glint in his eye or smirk that was a dead giveaway! As Mr. Morgan approached us he said that we would take the state car, and Mr. Carter said he'd drive.

Thad replied, "Oh no, I'll drive."

We loaded up and peeled out of there, and I do mean PEELED! We were well over the speed limit with Thad driving, David Carter trying to stay quiet, and me in the back getting tickled at the two of them. Finally, Mr. Carter, having gotten more nervous the further and faster we went, said "Now we don't want to get a ticket." Thad assured him that we couldn't get a ticket. The car had a blue tag!

By the four lanes in Troy we were creeping in on 80 miles per hour, David was in a wad in the front seat, and I was try-ing really hard not to let on how much I was enjoying the situation. When we got through Troy, it was obvious that we were not going to be late. Seeing this, David started to relax. I mean, the driving was hairy but at least we were on time.

About 10 miles south of Montgomery Thad said he wanted to stop for coffee at the Ponderosa. David volunteered to run in and get it, hoping I'm sure, to move it right along quickly. Thad Morgan was not having it. We all three went in and took a seat. You can imagine that Thad smirk. He absolutely knew what he was doing to David Carter's nerves. Thad ordered 3 cups of coffee.

David asked, "Shouldn't we get this to go?" to which Thad replied, "I can't drive with this coffee!" I tell you I watched David Carter drink that HOT coffee as fast as he could, and I do mean it was HOT! It was obvious to me that Mr. Carter was wound up and getting worse by the minute while Thad was sipping and chatting.

Mr. Carter said, "Shouldn't we go?"

Thad, three quarters of a cup left, said, "Let me finish my coffee!"

Mr. Carter didn't say another word even when we were leaving the Ponderosa at the approximate time that the meeting was to be starting, but he was beside himself! Thad knew it and was enjoying it, and it was all entertainment to me. Don't get me wrong, I am punctual and had it not been so dang funny watching it get off with David, I would have been much more wound up about being late to an event.

We pulled up obviously late, and Thad kindly let the two of

us out at the front door. It was like walking into church late. All of the back rows were full so we had to walk down to the front. LATE! At the State Department of Education! To be recognized for outstanding achievement! Poor David Carter had never had been late for anything in his life, and Thad enjoyed every second of this being the first time.

Of course Thad parked, sneaked in, and discreetly hung around until time to walk to the front with us to be recognized completely unfazed. Pure Thad Morgan!

Helping Students

I'm not exactly sure of the year, but it was the year that Bill Morgan was a senior and in my Fifth Year Math class. Thad was Principal of Enterprise High School and we all ate lunch together every day in the school cafeteria.

One day we sat down to eat, and Thad said, "Motes, we had an interesting conversation at supper last night."

I asked what about and his reply was "Your class!"

It hit me right about then what happened in the Fifth Year Math class the day before.

The Fifth Year class at that time consisted of the strongest math students at EHS. This was before AP Calculus. Most of these students were focused and sharp as tacks. There were two, however, who preferred to socialize instead of learn math. The class that day was working on some pretty difficult problems so I was working from the front of the room to the back answering questions for students.

As I started toward the two socialites, one of the boys said to the other, "Oh, here she comes. I thought she only helped foreigners and minorities."

Having heard the exchange, I replied, "No. son. I only help those who give a s**t!

At the lunch table that day Principal Morgan said he sure enjoyed hearing about class that night! I had not even thought about Bill being in the class at the time but Thad responded in typical supportive fashion.

He said, "Motes, let me tell you something. Don't you take no s**t off those two!"

This is an example of the support he always showed me through the course of my teaching career, and it was always appreciated.

Yvonne Jones

Mr. Morgan and I established a unique relationship over the many years I that I worked in the Enterprise School System. Many were much intimidated by his demeanor, but I learned very early on that he was simply a big teddy bear with lots of personality. We actually became neighbors. In fact, we lived three doors down from each other. When I walked past his house, I often caught him at the mailbox where we briefly chatted. When I retired in 2012, Mr. Morgan sent me a kind note which I still have, thanking me for my service to the Enterprise School System. One word fully describes Mr. Morgan – DEDICATION, to the very end!

Ed.'s Note: Below are the words Thad Morgan wrote to Yvonne when she retired from the Enterprise City School System.

Yvonne,

"Thank you for the job you have done for this school system and the children we serve.

I wish you the best in your retirement."

Thad Morgan

Mary Cannon

Beneath the scowl and growl and bark
There was a deeper part.
He was the wind beneath our wings
With a deeply caring heart.

I was blessed to know, work with, battle with, fear, respect and love Thad Morgan for more years than I can remember. I guess I was too old for his paddle but not for a corrective cussing. But what stands out most to me was his tender heart.

Thad loved the Lord, his church, his family, your family and the Wildcats. When his health allowed, Thad and Janice were always at church and sat near the back corner. He always wore a suit and tie selected by Janice. He loved the old hymns and shook his head but reluctantly accepted the drums, guitars, and more contemporary music. He held his much loved Janice's hand during every prayer.

Thad cared about everything going on in "his people's" families. If there was a sickness, death, or crisis – he was there to hug, love, and support "His people" including everyone in town. His prayers came from the heart.

Students with special needs held a special place in Mr. Morgan's heart. He would show up at our class at Hillcrest just to visit, stir up the students, and leave. During one visit, a much loved student cornered him with a complaint that Cannon was making her do multiplication. I was quickly told not to make Cindy multiply. I got the message. On another visit close to Christmas, he asked a student what she wanted Santa Claus to bring her. Her answer was "Santa Claus was an S.O.B."

Thad got the message.

I am very hesitant to share this last story, but here goes. A new wing was being added to Hillcrest right outside our classroom door. We created songs, stories, and rules about staying out of the way of construction workers and their equipment. Mr. Morgan also talked directly to the contractor and workers about safety and cussing.

The first day the jack hammers began tearing out bricks, one of our elder students with a colorful vocabulary went to the door and told the workers "You're waking up the babies and tearing down the f**king building!"

It didn't take long for Superintendent Morgan to arrive on the scene. I had never seen him laugh so hard. Throughout his administrative years, special education was a high priority with Mr. Morgan.

So many of our lives are better because of Thad Morgan. He was a legend in his own way. He made a difference.

Katheryn Price

Take It To Hell

During my 34 years of teaching, most of which Thad Morgan was my Principal and/or Superintendent, I encountered some strange people. However, one of the most unusual encounters involved a parent/teacher conference.

Mr. Z.I. Fleming, Assistant Principal, and Mr. Dan Pridgen, Counselor, arranged a parent/teacher conference with the parents of one of my students. The student was a good kid but was not very interested in Algebra II and spent more of his time on band than math. I was expecting a routine conference informing parents that more time should be spent on math homework and possibly a bit of after-school help. Little did I know what was to come!

Mr. Pridgen made the usual introductions and offered the father the opportunity to begin the conference. He immediately pointed his finger at Mr. Pridgen and then Mr. Fleming and shouted, "I did not want a conference with you, nor did I want a conference with him! I want a conference with her one-on-one!"

It took a moment for the "always calm" Mr. Pridgen to regain his composure. Finally, he replied, "This is our school policy. We always have counselors/administrators in conferences for the parents' protection as well as the teacher's."

The gentleman immediately jumped up and said, "I will take this to the Superintendent!"

My only thought was "GO, please!"

The next morning Mr. Carter, EHS Principal, met me as I reported to work. He told me that I should try to avoid this man if I encountered him in public. He informed me that Mr. Morgan had a very lengthy and heated discussion (yelling) with him the day before.

The gentleman ended his conversation with, "I will take this to the School Board!"

Mr. Morgan always had a way with words. He concluded the conversation with, "You can take it to the School Board, you can take it to the President, or you can take it to HELL!" The issue was resolved.

Crying Fat Man

When I was going through a divorce, I decided that I would tell Mr. Morgan that I was seeking extra work. I wanted him to know that I would not let it interfere with my job at EHS. AS we discussed my personal issues, tears filled my eyes.

He immediately replied, "Don't do that. Do you want to see a fat man cry?"

Underneath the tough exterior was a loving, caring man. He was one of a kind. I loved him for his support and help.

Joe Holley

To Walk With Us A Mile

College years were good to me. For nearly seven years of undergrad studies, I attended class almost regularly, took a few notes, and, on occasion, studied them to glean wisdom. Seven years is a long time to stay with undergraduate course-work, but my advanced diploma was built around a pragmatic approach. Taking unrelated courses that sounded interesting slowed progress, and changing majors four times did not help either.

During summer months it was my opportunity to work at Ridgecrest Baptist Assembly in the Blue Ridge Mountains near Asheville, North Carolina. Those were special times, 'serving the Lord' with over 500 college students as we ministered to thousands of guests from across the nation. It was at Ridgecrest that I came across a most relevant poem. I found it while going through an old college yearbook in our staff center. I do not remember the college, and the author was listed as 'unknown.' Anyway, the words were very meaningful, and I wrote them as a keepsake.

To WALK WITH Us A MILE

People come into our lives to walk with us a mile.
And then, because of circumstance, they only stay a while.
They chart the lanes of memory that move so quickly by
And then are gone beyond our reach, we often wonder why.
God only knows the reason why we meet and share a smile
Why people come into our lives to walk with us a mile.

My family moved to Enterprise during the mid-1960s. Enterprise was a much smaller community than it is today, and in those days, everyone in town was related. At the time, I was in the 10th grade and had lived all over the world. I had only one thing in common with my new contemporaries. It was something that my parents had ingrained in my heart for years . . . to care for others.

A tragedy had taken place prior to our arrival to Enterprise. It involved the family of a young man who was about my age. Being new to the community, I was not familiar with him or his family. I do remember the outpouring of love, care, and concern that I had for him. He was about my age, and I could only imagine the pain that the tragedy must have brought to him. I prayed that someday, I would meet him and become one of his friends.

After seven years in college, I had accumulated enough credits to earn an education degree, which meant that I could become a teacher. This was far from my original plan. Believe it or not, I had gone to college in order to become a famous entertainer. My mother was clear on the fact that I was about to go to work. That meant that I was about to become a teacher, and I just happened to be at the right place at the right time. My first placement was at Holly Hill Elementary School in Enterprise, Alabama.

Mr. Morgan (Thad) came to Enterprise City Schools at about the same time that I did. His original assignment was at Enterprise Junior High. Since I was an elementary teacher, our paths did not cross for a number of years. In time Mr. Morgan was hired as Principal at Enterprise High School and eventually became Superintendent of Enterprise City Schools.

My memory of Mr. Morgan is pleasant and varied. I remember him as a hard-working man filled with words, expectations, kindness, and a keen sense of humor. He was a man of words. Sometimes he had many, other times he had just a few. There were some that sounded a bit gruff, but most often, they were filled with love and encouragement. My initial acquaintance with Mr. Morgan took place when he was Principal at EHS, and it concerned football tickets. In those years I was the proud owner of 10 seats near the top of the reserved seat section.

When the Enterprise Wildcats made the football playoffs (for the first time) there was concern about how to manage ticket sales. It was determined that reserved ticket holders could get their tickets during the week from 8:00 and 3:30. It worked for most people, but being an instructor, getting to the high school before 3:30 was next to impossible. I went to get my 10 tickets but arrived at 3:40. The secretary told me that I was too late, but she sent me into Mr. Morgan's office anyway.

Mr. Morgan did not want to sell the tickets to me as it was too late in the day to sell them. He told me that I could wait in line like everyone else. Not meaning to be disrespectful, I pointed out how hard it was for teachers to get to the high school given the time constraints and told him that I did not want to wait in line. He responded that he did not want to mess up his book-keeping system.

His bookkeeping system just happened to be on his desk. It was a tackle box overflowing with tickets, checks, and cash. I looked at it, and he looked at it. He began to laugh, but he pulled my tickets and sold them to me. When his laughter subsided, he told me that he was very busy and that I needed to leave. I thanked him, shook his hand, and went my merry way.

In the following years Mr. Morgan became the Superintendent of Enterprise City Schools. I was still at Holly Hill Elementary. Believe it or not, I really enjoyed working with our youngsters. In those days, the central office staff would visit each class-room once each semester. They did not stay long, but they did want to touch base with every teacher.

The only drawback to my elementary classroom was the many bulletin boards. I had one that was four feet by four feet. Then, there were two that were four feet by twelve feet. Finally, there was a super large one that was four feet by thirty feet. Above each of these boards was a top board of one foot that extended the entire length of each board.

Bulletin board ideas came hard for me, but I did come up with many originals. One of my four by twelve boards had a red background with large white bubble letters. The letters spelled, BULLETIN BOARD, and each student had placed their autographs inside them.

When the central office staff came to my room, my bulletin boards featured science, social studies, and math. T hen, of course, there was the BULLETIN BOARD bulletin board. The staff visit went well. Mr. Morgan did pull me to the side to acknowledge my unusual creation. I thought that he might give negative comments. Instead, he said that it was one of the most creative bulletin boards that he had seen. He laughed, I laughed, and we went about our business.

I moved to Coppinville Junior High in the late 1980s in order to teach a computer course to all of our seventh graders. It was during the years when computer technology was beginning to expand everywhere. In those days most of our school computers were the Apple IIe, the ones with the large floppy disks.

As time passed, Enterprise City Schools accumulated a large number of these machines, and it became necessary to find a way to service and clean each machine during the summer months. Mr. Morgan decided that I was to be sent to school in order to learn this skill.

For many summers servicing ECS computers was my part-time job. It was during these summer months that I came to realize how much work took place at each of our schools during vacation months. Grounds keeping, building maintenance, and servicing of vehicles played a major part in making Enterprise City Schools clean and safe.

Mr. Morgan took a special interest in our son, Josh. He sent Josh along with me to make sure that the job was done correctly. At one point, Josh told Mr. Morgan that every school in the system was clean and spotless. Mr. Morgan thanked Josh for his compliment and told him that Enterprise City Schools was a 19 million dollar operation and had to be properly maintained for safety and cleanliness.

Eventually, there were over 1500 computers in our schools. That was quite a few machines for just one person to manage during summer work alone. It was at that point that I suggested that it might be time to employ a regular technician (and it did not have to be me) that could dedicate their full attention to maintaining all of the computers throughout the school year. The idea did not receive a favorable response from Mr. Morgan so we dropped the subject.

In later years, Mr. Morgan had to deal with a few health issues. They were serious, but he stayed very active in spite of it. His memory was quite keen during this time, and when we would meet at local businesses, he would always stop and ask about our family. Each time he would remind me about his love for Josh and how much he missed our son. For the record, Josh lived a normal life for 25 years. He never missed a school day due to illness. He never displayed any health problems. He was an active young man and worked his way through college on an athletic scholarship. Two months before his 25th birthday he had a health condition that the doctors could not fix. He passed to the Lord on Good Friday of 2003 and was buried on Easter Sunday afternoon. Mr. Morgan was one of the many people in attendance for Josh's funeral.

It has been a journey, one that has charted many memories. I am thankful for the miles that Thad and our family have shared over the years. I do miss him, but I look forward to the day when we shall meet again on the other side.

Buena Snellgrove

One of the things I remember about working with Thad is one day during the summer months he came over to my room and office on fourth hall at the high school and asked if I had seen the new elementary school – Harrand Creek. I said no I had not been over to see it so he said come on and we will get Becky (Distributive Education Coordinator) and I'll take y'all over to see it.

Thad was very proud of the new school and was excited to show it to anyone. So we got Becky and got in Thad's old blue Oldsmobile (I think that was the color and make) to go over to the new school. When we got to the bypass I thought maybe I should have taken my car and when we got to the four lanes at Rucker Boulevard, it was even scarier. We made it to Harrand Creek and back to the high school fine, but it was a wild ride. I kept thinking and remembering that Thad used to teach Driver Education at Enterprise High School.

When Thad was Principal at Enterprise High School and sometimes even as Superintendent, he would visit my class-room unannounced. When he came in the door I would think he had come to speak to me, but that was not the case. He would motion for me to continue with my lesson. Although he would stay only a minute, he wanted me as a teacher and the students to know he was very visible throughout the building and that he liked to just pop into the classroom periodically.

He occasionally brought visitors around with him.

Several of us teachers who had second lunch would often eat our lunch in the teachers' lounge. Some of us would have fifth period planning right after lunch. As we were waiting for the halls to clear to go to our classrooms, we would hear several big knocks on the lounge door. The first time it startled us, but then we became accustomed to the knocks and knew it was Mr. Morgan. He called that group of five teachers the fifth period Mafia.

Tracy Kyser

I came to know (I shudder to say "Thad Morgan" - he will forever be "Mr. Morgan" to me) on both a personal and professional level. Since childhood he was often mentioned in our home mainly because his housekeeper and sitter for his daughter was Mrs. Gussie Trawick. Gussie was my grandmother Ethyl Kyser's very best friend. "Miss Gussie" absolutely adored Thad whom she always called "Thadius."

Miss Gussie used to mention him a lot in our front porch conversations. It was always good. She had a great abundance of love and respect for Mr. Morgan and "Miss Janice." Mr. Morgan helped her get her driver's license and got her first, and to my knowledge, only car. I think it was one of his old cars he handed down to her. Come to think of it, he may have helped her get her two cars- I can't quite remember so Mr. Morgan was always a household name in our family long before I ever dreamed of working for him.

Mr. Morgan had a presence about him to whom few can compare. He was kind but stern, the kind of stern that instantly garnered respect. He was always intimidating to me but never in a bullish way. When he entered a room, the attention immediately turned to him. He immediately took leadership of a room full of people upon entering whether they knew him or not.

He had the type of personality that instantly instilled a sense of confidence in people that their leader had arrived. He was not arrogant. Never. But he possessed a kind of "tooth sucking" air about him that made one feel as if he knew what he was talking about – and he did know! He possessed an abundance of what eludes people – the traits of common sense and rectitude. Mr. Morgan just knew...whatever it was, he just knew or knew how to find out!

He was honest, trustworthy, and kind but direct, candid, blunt, and certain.

I have used Mr. Morgan as my template for mastering these traits in my own life.

My personal beginnings were rather austere. Although my family had for generations been a necessary part of Enterprise history, we had never been the doctors, lawyers, teachers or bankers. I have no noteworthy fruit hanging from my family tree. My folks were farmers, laborers, weavers, loom fixers and the like. We were very common folk! But we did stay out of trouble and paid our bills. My father and sister were the first in my long Enterprise family history to graduate high school. But from an early age my dream was to be a teacher.

It was meant to be! And not just a teacher but a teacher in Enterprise! So I went on to be the first in the family to graduate college.

When I applied for a position at Enterprise High School in the 1980s, there was actually a teacher surplus. In Enterprise City Schools in those days teachers were required to teach 30 years to reach retirement eligibility, and the teacher turnover in the system was very slow. So I had to wait two years for an opening and then had to compete with dozens of candidates for the first opening in the high school history department in a dozen or so years.

As the number of candidates for the position was finally reduced to a handful of eager newbies, I was directed to meet with Mr. Morgan. I was dressed in my best, eager as a beaver, and livelier than a squirrel – but was scared to death and "quaking in my boots." Mr. Morgan was very direct in his questions to me – loud and stern. I had no doubt he was in charge.

After several minutes of questions and chatting a bit, he stuck out his hand and said, "I'm offering you this job at the high school. Do you want it?"

I said, "Yes, of course!" He then went on a few more minutes giving me instructions on whom to meet with to fill out all the necessary paperwork, work scheduling, etc. I was excited but petrified!

Finally, he asked, "Any questions from you?'

Staring at my shoes, I asked, "Do you mind my asking what the salary is?"

Mr. Morgan laughed strongly and loudly and said, "Hell, Son, that should have been the first thing you asked me!"

He pulled a sheet of the salary matrix from his desk drawer (we weren't using computers yet) and said, "$16,854.00!"

I was in heaven. I had just played the lottery and won. Mr.

Morgan had given me my first chance to be somebody. I was not going to let him down!

Mr. Morgan continued to follow my career with the Enterprise City Schools even after his retirement. He was very proud of me – and that meant something.I went on to get my Master's Degree and eventually my Doctorate from Auburn University, being one of the few classroom teachers in our system to earn it. As I begin year 38 with EHS, I will be looking up at the Heavens, knowing he is looking down with love and pride he had for all of us!

FINAL THOUGHT

One time Mr. Morgan's physician scheduled him to receive a prostate exam. At the completion of the exam, the doctor handed him some tissue. Mr. Morgan immediately responded, "Is this to wipe my a** or to wipe my eyes?"

I'm going to miss your frank humor, Mr. Morgan.

Hilda Allen

My full name is Hilda Culver Allen. I am married to Tim Allen. All my married life I have heard tales of Coach Thad Morgan. You see, he was Tim's coach in Junior High School and when his class "graduated" to high school they thought they were leaving Coach Morgan behind but upon reaching those hallowed halls, low and behold Coach Morgan had "graduated" with them. So I knew about the man long before I met the man. The couple of stories I will relate here are stories that others can tell about and probably do it so much more eloquently, but here goes.

In July of 1988 I decided to leave corporate employment and seek employment with Enterprise City Schools. My good friend Kathy Wilson had become employed with the schools in the Central Office the year before and contacted me when an opening became available for me to pursue. I interviewed with Mr. Charles Howell, the Assistant Superintendent. When he called back a few days later I was elated. This interview was to be with him and Mr. Morgan in Mr. Morgan's office. Anyone who had ever been to the old Central Office will know what I am about to describe.

You had to go down a couple of steps to get to his office and there was a sofa in front of his desk. I didn't realize at the time until I sat down that sitting there put you below eye level of the person sitting at the desk. I felt small. Now this is tough for me not only because of my personality but because I am an Amazon in statue (5 feet and 11 inches). I always thought that seating arrangement in his office was by design.

Mr. Morgan told me that day that he had reservations about hiring me for the receptionist job because I was over qualified. I think he was taken aback when I told him that I wanted to work for the school system even if it was to sweep the floors. I must have made an impression. I started to work in the Central Office as the receptionist on August 2, 1988.

That first week of working there was rather tough for me. I had to not only learn all the different people working in the Central Office but all the other administrators in the school system and where their titles put them in respect to the school but had to learn how the phone system worked. You see, I had come from an accounting background. I am a "bean counter." To make things even tougher, the second Monday of my employment there was a new phone system to learn that had been installed over the weekend.

The morning was going pretty well until I experienced my first phoned in bomb threat. Needless to say I was shaken. I will never forget sitting in Mr. Morgan's office with the police trying to exactly remember what was said and any other sounds that had come over on the phone. It seemed that Mr. Morgan was so calm. Like this kind of thing happened all the time. Wow. And this was my first full week of work. I wondered if things could get any worse. They did.

I've provided the above description of my first few days working in the Central office in order to lead up to my first real experience of watching Mr. Morgan "at his finest." On Friday morning of this particular week, there were many rumblings down the hall towards the breakroom as the day was beginning.

Shortly Mr. Morgan came stomping up the hall going into his office. I wondered what was going on. This had not been the normal behavior in the mornings. In a few seconds he came out of his office and up those couple of steps jerking off his tie and slinging it onto the file cabinets that lined one wall. He had his paddle in his hand. He was saying "I'll teach them to want to make a statement."

He exited the Central Office out the side door that led to the high school. We did not know that the football team had decided to wear "head rags" as some sort of statement prior to their first game of the season. Mr. Morgan had proceeded over to the high school and had found each one of those players and paddled them.

I distinctly remember him as he was coming back into the Central Office later that morning. He still had the paddle in his hand and was saying something to the effect of "Man, that felt good" as he picked up his tie and retired to his office.

Now remember, I had come from corporate employment where employees worked at their respective desks all day and hardly ever even interacted.

I was wondering if I had jumped from the frying pan and into the fire. But as the weeks and years clicked by, I knew I had truly become part of a "family." I especially loved to listen to Mr. Morgan when we all sat around talking about old times. He along with Jerlon Godwin, Child Nutrition Supervisor and Joanne Grimsley, school nurse could relate some "good ole tales" from times gone by. Eloise Carrol, Anita Crutchfield and Gladys Welch had also worked with him for a very long time. Gladys had been his secretary when he was the principal at the high school. The Central Office staff was truly like family.

And as with most families, kindly jokes were played on each other from time to time. One I remember especially well was around Christmas time. That year Brenda Weakley, the elementary supervisor at the time had been given a water pistol. She was having a large time squirting all of us with it. She had gone into Jim Reese's office and I think Bob Phares maybe was in there too.

I knew they were getting a dose of the water gun when Mr. Morgan came by the front of my desk with the water pitcher from the coffee pot in the breakroom. He had evidently already gotten his "shot" of the water gun. As Brenda was exiting Jim's office, he poured the entire pitcher of water on Brenda's head. Not a single person got mad. We all behaved like family having fun.

This was for the most part normal behavior for our staff. We played hard but we also worked hard. In 1998 I moved from that part of the Central Office to the newly constructed Service Center. During my 27 years with the school system, I worked with many, many administrators, teachers and other employees but those years in the old office with Mr. Morgan and the original group were precious memories.

Several years after I had retired from the school system, I went to visit Mr. Morgan when he was in the hospital in Enterprise one afternoon. Janice had been taken home by Marcia Tomberlin to get some rest. Mr. Morgan and I had a very deep conversation that afternoon. Rarely do two people get that opportunity nowadays. I came away from that short visit that afternoon knowing that in a person's life there are people that truly make a difference in your life and you make a difference in their lives. Mr. Morgan might have seemed to be a little rough around the edges, but he was truly a great man to a great number of people. I am a better person for knowing him.

Susie Strickland

My mama went to school with Mr. Morgan throughout all their school years so I've known about Thad and how much he meant to his classmates. Mama also had the privilege of working with him for more years than I know. Although Mama is suffering from early signs of dementia, she still says, "He was one of my very best friends" whenever his name is mentioned. He was truly a loyal friend not only to her but to many others.

When the EF4 tornado came through Enterprise on March 1, 2007, Mr. Morgan immediately came out of retirement and was there to do whatever was needed of him. This was heartbreaking for Enterprise and my family. Mama lost a grandson during the tornado. Mr. Morgan prayed for us, cried with us, laughed with us and cared for us with love and compassion. I must add that all the administrators of the Enterprise City School System were overwhelmingly supportive of not only our family but the other seven families who lost children during the tornado. My family will never forget how well we were loved and cared for!

I was an employee of the Enterprise School System for 29 years working in the Special Education Department. Our students lacked for nothing. This was due to the leadership and support of Mr. Morgan. One of his favorite things was the interaction with our special education students. He loved all of his students and made sure they were provided a quality education and treated with respect. He expected the same respect from the students toward the teachers and school staff. I guess this is a good place to add that he believed in discipline. Yes, he could and would swing that board! Thankfully, I never experienced the feeling of being paddled.

One incident I remember happened during a Special Education Graduation Ceremony at Hillcrest Elementary School. Mr. Morgan was in attendance and was seated about midway down the auditorium in an aisle seat. As a female graduate was walking down the aisle to receive her diploma, she stopped and kissed Mr. Morgan on top of his head. He took it like a champ! I feel sure that the student was coached to do that by her teachers Mary Cannon and Karen Bowden.

Mr. Morgan treated employees like family. He would personally visit every retiring employee and thank them for their time and dedication to the Enterprise City Schools. At least I remember him doing that for me.

Who can forget Coach walking the sidelines at every football game? He was definitely a Wildcat. This was probably the thing he loved most.

If I could choose two words to describe Mr. Morgan, they would be LOYAL and DEDICATED!

Cindy Piggott

The subject of Mr. Morgan's skin cancer came up one day as we were talking in the break room. He told me they had to take a place off his nose and do a skin graft. The color of the skin replaced was darker than the rest of his skin on his face. He told me it was because the skin graft came from Coach Peavy's ass.

I always respected Mr. Morgan but also learned that he had a caring and tender heart. The day I signed my letter of intent to transfer from College Street Elementary School to the Superintendent's Office as a secretary, he slid the letter to me on the desk but held it, looked at me and said, "Before you sign this letter, know the family comes first." He was very concerned and supportive during those few times that they did. Mr. Morgan will always hold a special place in my heart and will never be forgotten.

I know there are so many more memories out there and so many people he touched in many ways (paddle or no paddle).

Judy Williams

One day in mid 1986, I was strolling my fussy infant on a small running track behind Hillcrest Elementary School. As we were making our way around the track, we were approached by a nice man dressed in office attire with his necktie loosened, and he cordially introduced himself and leaned down to speak to my cranky infant in his stroller. My baby immediately stopped fussing and awarded him a big toothless smile. The nice man was Mr. Thad Morgan whom I had never met, and being new in town did not know that he was the Superintendent of Schools.

Years later when our second child entered kindergarten, I decided to return to work to continue my employment and add to my years toward retirement. I found myself across Mr. Morgan's desk accepting an invitation from Dr. Mike Cutchen to work for him at Pinedale Elementary School. I remembered the kind man I had met at the walking trail years before.

Three years later Mr. Morgan invited me to come to work for him at the Central Office in Payroll and Accounting. Working closely with Mr. Morgan gave me an opportunity to see the genuine talents and caring heart of this man. His brilliant financial mind, his respect for all employees and children were some of the traits that I came to admire and appreciate. His sincere empathy for employees who were facing adversity and employee's family member facing a heartbreaking diagnosis or the needs of a child are examples of Mr. Morgan's compassion.

I experienced his compassion first hand years later when our 10 year old son tragically died. He made it a point to check on me regularly at work, and we had many conversations about his daughter Bitsy who also had died in the month of June. By sharing his grief, he helped me to cope with mine and encouraged me to continue my journey. I retired after 17 years of service with the Enterprise City Schools, and my last conversation with Mr. Morgan was at Enterprise Health and Rehab where he was staying a short time to recover from a fall. The conversation centered around my being on his "A" team for the Central Office and what a great run we had. He told me that he was ready to go home and he was not referring to Tartan Pines...but with the Lord. We both shed tears, said goodbyes and as I closed the door, he told me that he would be looking for me.

I am sincerely grateful for the years of working with Mr. Morgan and all the lessons learned.

Employee with the Enterprise City Schools 1994-2011

Paulie Thill

I was asked to write a few words on how I remembered Mr. Thad Morgan. I worked as a paraprofessional for the Special Education Department at Hillcrest School. My principal was Mr. Hugh Williams whom I have always admired and respected. It was mandatory for the principal to take the new hire in to meet the superintendent for a brief interview before being recommended to be hired.

I was a bit nervous because of all the rumors I had heard about this man and how intimidating he could be. As soon as we walked into his office, he stood up like a giant and started pointing his finger at Mr. Williams and yelling explicative verbs right and left while looking at me. After he finished expressing himself, they shook hands and both were grinning. I must say my future boss had a very red face, and I was ready to run! At the end of the interview I was welcomed kindly into my future teaching job.

Mr. Morgan was known as an authoritarian who played a major force in our school system whether it was managing finances, hiring and firing personnel, , and being the biggest and best fan of the ENTERPRISE WILDCATS. I can still close my eyes and see him running up and down the sidelines coaching.

I was always humbled by Mr. Morgan's love for our special needs students. His whole disposition would change when he saw them perform or walk into our classroom. He loved to hear Dennis Pierson sing "Precious Lord." It never failed to see his tears stream down his face with a white handkerchief to dry them up. Our special education teachers, aides, para-professionals, and nursing staff were blessed to see the true side of this man others would never experience. Mr. Morgan had a big heart and was very compassionate not only for our students but the entire student body and Enterprise City School System. A legend in his time indeed!

RIP Mr. Morgan

Mandy Waters

I had the privilege of working with Mr. Morgan when I started at the Board of Education in 2007 when he came out of retirement after the tornado. My two girls were in kindergarten and 1st grade at the time so after school they would come to my work until I got off.

It wasn't long until Mr. Morgan learned that they loved Skittles so almost daily he would hand them each a bag when they got out of school. If Mr. Morgan had already left for the day, I would return to work with Jules and Riley to find two small brown bags with their Skittles inside placed in my chair.

He had a love of children, and it warmed my heart that he cared so much for mine. I had always heard of the "gruff" Mr. Morgan but during my time with him, I listened to his stories and how he would quickly help someone in need or set them straight as needed.

As the years passed he would stop by work to give everyone a hard time and a few laughs. He never failed to ask about my family and how "the girls" were doing. One day he said to me, "I pray for you and your girls every day. I do."

I don't think he knew how much those words meant to me and still do.

A few days prior to his passing Jules, working as a paramedic, got a call to his home. Once a little girl he brought Skittles to, now grown into a young woman, was caring for him. I truly loved Mr. Morgan and will always treasure my time with him. The stories and memories he shared will never be forgotten. Thad Morgan is truly a LEGEND!

Central Office /
System Administrators

Tim Alford
(AKA The Word Man)

Sketches of My Life with Thadius William Morgan
THE BEGINNING

I first met Thad at the Enterprise Country Club where Enterprise businessman Billy Hildreth was hosting his annual fish fry for area athletic coaches and school officials whose schools patronized his sporting goods store. At the time I had been the Principal (using that term loosely) of Opp Middle School. Although the athletic equipment purchases, as well as all other purchases, were negligible at my little school, my Superintendent J.L. Nolen and Assistant Superintendent Raymond Chisum had invited me to attend the fish fry. Having an active three-year-old son at home along with a wife who was five months pregnant with our daughter, I, of course, pondered for a good while (approximately three seconds) before I accepted the invitation.

My superiors and I drove over together and joined in with the food and socialization. At some point well into the activities, a gentleman who was a stranger to me, walked up and in a loud and gruff voice asked, "You Tim Alford?" A little startled, I responded, "Yes sir, I am."

"I hear you can read 'n write, that so?"

"I guess so—at least if the words aren't too big."

He went on, "Well, I'm gonna be the new Principal of Enterprise High School next school year and I need somebody that can read and write. You interested in talking to me about it?"

"Well, I'm not looking for a job, but I'll be glad to discuss possibilities with you."

"Can you come to Enterprise next Friday? I wanna talk to you."

"Yes sir. Just say when and where."

"Come to the high school office at around nine o'clock."

"Yes sir."

THE INTERVIEW

Later, Raymond Chisum, my friend and Assistant Superintendent at Opp, told me he knew Thad from Auburn and that he had recommended me to him, knowing that opportunities for advancement would be better in the Enterprise School System. I went to the high school the next Friday morning as planned. Half scared to death, I, of course, arrived early and was sent across the hall to Mr. Morgan's office. When I got there, his door was closed and I was told he was busy, so his secretary directed me to have a seat in the outer office.

After a short while, Thad and a large black man, whom I didn't know, burst out of the office, apparently angry and in the midst of some heated argument. I didn't know anything to do but sit there and try not to look as scared as I was. I don't remember much that was said but I will never forget that at some point in the proceedings, Thad said, "I ought to put you back to pickin' cotton." The undeterred black man responded, "You white folks done got too sorry to even grow cotton, so where you gonna put me to pickin'?" I thought I was about to see a full- fledged, knock-down, drag-out fight.

Then they both laughed, slapped each other on the back and Thad introduced me to the iconic Assistant Principal known as Coach Peavy. I shook his hand and told him my name and he smiled and responded, "Nice to meet you. Don't pay any attention to our carrying on."

Thad said, "Come on. We'll go over to the meeting room so we can talk without being interrupted." We went across the hall to a relatively large room arranged as a group meeting area. Thad pulled out the end chair and motioned me to have a seat. He then pulled his chair over right up against mine and leaned over within a couple of inches of my face. Adopting an adversarial pose, he blurted out in a loud voice, "I know you're not interested in this job. You're just over here to get a raise in Opp."

I didn't know what to say. I was intimidated but I managed to respond in a shaky voice, "Mr. Morgan, I'm here at your invitation but I'll leave if you think I'm wasting your time."

"Hey, good response, I like that!" he replied, smiling. "Sit back down and let's talk."

We did discuss particulars and during our discussion, the bell rang for a class change. He stood up, motioned to me, and said, "Come on, walk down to the cafeteria with me." I dutifully followed and we inched our way through the shoulder-to-shoulder mass of students navigating their way to their next class. They interacted with "Mr. Morgan" and many of them courteously spoke to me and I responded.

We came back to the meeting room and Thad admitted that he had no business at the cafeteria. "I just wanted to see how you'd react to the students. You seem at ease with them. I like that. I had another candidate for the job in here the other day and we took the same walk and I think he was scared to death. And by the way, I've checked you out and I'm offering you this job if you really want it but please don't waste my time. I've got a lot to do in a short time before school starts in the fall."

I had checked on Enterprise schools too and I responded immediately, "I want the job, but I need to talk to my wife before officially accepting if that's all right."

"Wouldn't want it any other way. Take all the time you need as long as you call me by Monday."

A few days after I had accepted the job and discussed it with my Opp employers, my wife Freddie, who was about to burst with our baby, and I scheduled a trip to Enterprise to meet with Thad and look for a house to rent. My car quit about half way there. All I knew to do was call Thad. He came and picked us up at a farm house near where my car stopped. A kind lady had let us use her phone to call Thad and had taken pity on Freddie in the heat and invited us to wait inside her house.

Thad picked us up and sent a man over to repair our car. Thad had a house picked out for us to check out and we rented it and soon began our life in Enterprise. Our daughter Alyson was born on October 15.

MY FIRST DAY

I reported for duty at the high school on the first Monday in August. I expected a day of orientation and discussion of expectations. Instead, I walked into Thad's office and he said, "Hey, New Boy, there's a group of teachers down in the library who are about to meet to revise the student handbook. Go down there and see if you can help."

I sheepishly asked, "Where is the library?" And Thad responded. "First left down the hall, big room, you can't miss it."

I hesitantly joined a group of ladies seated around a table and with a cracking voice, I nervously introduced myself. "Good morning, I'm Tim Alford, one of the new assistant principals."

The group was already underway with their revisions so one of the ladies tossed me a student handbook from the previous year and they proceeded with their page-by-page review. I said nothing. As they approved the last page, English teacher Louise Williamson asked if I had any suggestions. I reluctantly pointed out one spelling error that had gone unnoticed in the previous year's edition. They dismissed and exited down the hallway in front of the main office.

As they walked down the hall by Thad's office, he came out and asked the group, "Y'all meet the new boy? Has he got any sense?" To which a veteran teacher who had taught Thad when he was in school, Ms. Thelma Martin, responded, "He's got enough sense to keep his mouth shut which is more than I can say about you." Ms. Williamson then added, "You'll be glad to know he caught a couple of errors your English teachers missed." I knew at that point that this new job was gonna be a hell of a ride—-and it was!

Despite this inauspicious beginning, Thad and I spent five successful years working together at the high school. During that time, Thad and the entire faculty and staff were great to me personally and they were extremely cooperative in the academic initiatives we sought to employ. My fellow assistant principals David Carter and Coach Peavy became like brothers to me and Louise Williamson, by her own admission, became my second mother. Margie Watson was my secretary, advisor, and confidant. Strong personal friendships developed with counselor Dan Pridgen, art teacher Julian Thompson, French teacher Claude Bauer and history teacher Rex Bryan.

All the professional friendships that developed are too many to name here but, I must at least mention the teachers' "3rd Period Planning Mafia" as a group. There was one guy who taught psychology and sociology who came from his classroom to my office every day at his break for the purpose of completing the crossword puzzle in the newspaper which also came to my office. He was Jim Reese and he became not only a lifelong close friend but also the successor to Thad as Superintendent of the Enterprise City Schools.

Space does not allow me to tell all the great things that went on at Enterprise High School during the five years I was there with Thad. Under his leadership, as well as that of David Carter, Alfred Peavy and all the faculty and staff, great achievements were made by a group of outstanding teachers and students. Things went so well that the faculty even began to refer to the High School as Camelot. I once said that we had so many outstanding students at once that it tended to make you believe in astrology.

I can't start naming names of students or teachers because neither space nor my waning memory is sufficient to do so. I do remember teachers who gave up their free periods and lunch times to coach math teams, coaches who worked on Saturdays and Sundays, teachers who taught an extra class for no additional compensation so students could take an advanced course, teachers and parents who worked the concession stands at every athletic event to help provide funds for debate teams or band or school plays or yearbooks or math tournaments or ROTC or color guard or cheerleaders or on and on and on.

The students won state and sometimes national championships in athletics, band, mathematics, ROTC, debate, vocational education, FBLA, public speaking, foreign languages, cheerleading, and in other areas I am sure I don't recall at this moment. In the midst of all this, recognizing, encouraging, and often aggravating them, was the omnipresent Thad Morgan.

Fun Recollections of Thad – EHS

In our first week, we managed to get school started and began planning for the first football game which was on the road at Selma High School. Thad was a nervous wreck. He decided that he should stand on the sideline at a distance away from the coaches and players. He didn't ask but we assistant principals agreed. Someone asked me at the game if I thought Thad might interfere with the new coach. I responded, "Absolutely not."

"Then why does he want to be on the field?"

"Because he is so worked up, he might start fighting anybody that made a derogatory remark about a play selection or a player's execution of it, or the band's music selections."

Thad did get in a little trouble and learned an important lesson at the game. While standing on the sideline, he did continue to loudly question the calls of the officials. Finally, one official stopped the action, came over to Thad and yelled, "Sir, if you are a coach or affiliated with the team, I am going to penalize the team 15 yards for unsportsmanlike conduct."

Thad quickly responded, "Oh, no sir, I'm the bus driver." The referee answered, "Well, pipe down!" There was no penalty.

My written description can never fully describe what I consider to be one of the best examples of Thad's unique methods of dispensing discipline and punishment. To understand this particular example, one should first know that Thad did not allow boys or men who were not in school to come onto the campus or parking lots during lunch. For good reason, he did not want current high school female students to visit with their older boyfriends who had graduated or dropped out. With this in mind, Thad asked us assistants to stop by the cafeteria and parking lot at lunch when our schedules permitted. He did the same.

On one such occasion, I was headed toward the football field parking lot when I saw Thad had preceded me. He had already spotted a former male student who was sitting in his car in the parking lot waiting for his girlfriend to join him during her lunch time. Thad had asked this young man to leave on a previous occasion so when Thad began to approach the boy, he started his car and proceeded to back out of the parking space and take off across the parking lot.

At the time, Thad took great pride in driving an old ragged out white pickup truck with a bad manual gear shift. Thad jumped into his truck to chase the boy down before he got away, but he couldn't get his gear shift into forward drive. To solve the problem, Thad put his old truck in reverse, opened the driver's door so he could turn and see toward the rear and took off in reverse at full speed. As I watched, Thad chased the boy first around the parking lot and then out into the street behind the high school, all the while still driving in reverse at high speeds. The boy turned onto the street behind the elementary school and increased his speed. Thad followed in an equally high speed except he was still hanging out the door flying backwards. The two speedsters disappeared down Henderson Street, headed toward downtown. After a few minutes passed, I started back toward the office. Before I left, I turned back toward the street and got a glimpse of Thad slowly returning, still in reverse, but with the satisfaction that he had caught his man in town and he would not be back to the high school at lunch break again.

Later on that year, we all made a mistake waiting almost too long to dismiss school and get all the students and staff home before the arrival of Hurricane Eloise. All the buses and student cars made it home safely but I had to go in my back door to get into our house because tree limbs were already covering the front entrance when I got home. We had many people who left the Gulf Coast and came to Enterprise and stayed in our National Guard Armory. However, the storm was much worse in Enterprise than on the coast and there was a lot of damage.

On a more serious level, in order to illustrate students' love for Thad, I am reminded of a hot summer day when I was standing just outside my office and saw a group of black high school students standing outside the building beyond Thad's office. My curiosity peaked, and I looked to see what was going on. This group of young men had walked all the way from their houses across town in the hot August weather just to visit Mr. Morgan. The young men knew better than to just burst into Thad's office. They also knew that Mr. Morgan had a strict policy of not allowing males to wear hats inside the school. First offense of the hat rule resulted in one strong and truly hurtful lick from Mr. Morgan's big board. Failure to say an immediate "thank you" to Thad resulted in a second strong lick from his "board of education."

As I watched this group of boys, I came to realize that the older students had walked over some of the younger guys who would be first-year high school students in a few weeks when school started.

The entire group only had one hat with them, so they were standing outside and taking turns putting the same hat on and then walking individually inside to Mr. Morgan's office to be discovered wearing a hat. They then received the appropriate stern lick from Mr. Morgan's paddle. None of them ever said, "Thank you, sir" quickly enough to avoid the second lick and I mean these were hard licks from a big paddle. Even so, they each in turn put on the hat and marched into the office.

I'm not sure the young men would describe it this way, but I believe they were there to see Mr. Morgan and receive a paddling because (1) they missed Thad's attention during the summer and (2) they also wanted to initiate their first-year younger brothers and friends. These and other students loved to interact with Mr. Morgan—even if it meant getting hit by his paddle, which was viewed by many as a badge of distinction.

In addition to initiating his male students, Thad helped them in many ways, including loaning them money. He also put them to work earning the money back, and he deployed the board if they failed to do so. Though he would never admit it, he did it all out of love for his students.

One Friday afternoon, Thad asked me if I'd like to ride down to his beach house and back with him on Saturday. He said he had a little work to do and just wanted to check on things. Thinking that he might want to talk about something that was school related, I asked him what time he wanted to leave. He said, "I'll pick you up at your house at eight."

He arrived right on time the next morning but, to my surprise, he had a former student of his with him. The young man took the middle of the seat between Thad and me, and we drove to Panama City Beach. Thad introduced me to the young man and told me he was a former student who was gonna do a little work for him at the beach house.

The young man said nothing for the major portion of the trip as Thad and I intermittently engaged in insignificant small talk. Somewhere, well past the Florida line, the young man asked out of the blue, "the wodo woll?" Then Thad said, "Speak plain, I can't tell what you're saying. Say it slow."

The young man tried to oblige, "The Wota Roll?"

"Oh," Thad said, "He's asking me does the water roll at the beach."

We got to Thad's beach house and he got the young man to mow the small amount of grass. Then Thad took him across the street and down to the beach so he could take off his shoes and dabble in the water and "watch the water roll."

We had hamburgers on the way home and talked about school stuff until Thad dropped me off. As I had partially figured out, Thad told me Monday afternoon after work that the young man was a former special education student that he helped out occasionally by paying him for some light yard work.

"Somewhere along the way," Thad said, "I found out he had never been to the beach in his life. Thought it was about time for him to go."

Thad might talk to some of his students like "a dog," but he also on rare occasions, got one of them out of jail and out of other predicaments, and helped them earn a little "walking around money" when needed. He would never admit it, but he would even counsel with them like a loving father as long as nobody was watching.

I have mentioned examples of Thad's relationships with economically disadvantaged students, but he employed the same tactics and got the same results with the most economically advantaged students.

MOVING TO THE SUPERINTENDENT'S OFFICE

In 1979, Mr. Jack Rutland announced his retirement as Enterprise Superintendent and Thad was the only name I heard as a possible successor, and he was certainly the sole candidate for us high school folks. Shortly after it became official that Thad was the new superintendent, he asked me to come to his office and proceeded to tell me that he wanted me to "go across the walkway" with him. He told me that David Carter would be the new principal with Jim Reese taking his former position and Coach Peavy remaining as an assistant principal. Of course, these were all great choices who had contributed to the excellence at the high school.

I settled in as leader of federal programs and instruction, with Ms. Jennie Lind Coe assisting with elementary instruction. I was still what Thad called his "word man," helping with writing speeches and letters, developing school board agendas, keeping school board minutes, etc. I also occasionally had the unofficial task of standing between Thad and disgruntled male parents, especially early on in his superintendency. There was hardly a day that Thad and I and often others didn't start the day off before business hours in the break room and end it in the late afternoon in his office. Our relationship grew even stronger. We sometimes disagreed on an issue, but we never actually argued and I always knew who the boss was.

As happened while we were at the high school, we later had another threat of a coastal storm that was said to possibly be coming our way. Remembering our previous close call, we declared all schools closed for the next day and took all the usual precautions with buses, buildings, etc. We got to the office as planned about daylight the next morning. The sun arose to a beautiful, totally calm, sunshiny day. We spent most of the day hosting guests and friends throughout the city who CAME by our office with umbrellas and rainwear to rag us about our mistake. They offered us the use of their storm shelters, basements, flashlights, and heavy equipment. In the meantime, we walked around and enjoyed a beautiful day.

One of the highlights of this period to me came during one Christmas vacation when I convinced our secretary, Gladys Welch (AKA Bad Gladys), to give up some of her Christmas vacation time to do the clerical work for me to submit a proposal for the high school to be selected and honored as one of the first High Schools of Distinction in the nation, in a recognition started by President Reagan.

The competition was based on all facets of school including academic excellence and national test scores, student honors and awards, athletics and so forth. Enterprise High School was one of the first national selections. It was a thrill for Thad and me to learn that one of our schools was in the first group selected in the nation. The recognition and leadership of David Carter, Jim Reese, Alfred Peavy and the entire faculty and staff were well deserved and we were thrilled for them. We were also thrilled our elementary and junior high schools had played an equally important role in getting them there. But the overall leadership in achieving this award and all the others won by the schools found its way back to Thad.

Thad and I had an interesting venture when we made our first trip to Washington for the Impact Aid annual meeting. Our schools received significant funds from the federal program which was designed to provide offset funding for tax revenue not realized because of the presence of tax-free military bases, and to support the cost associated with educating the military's children.

Of course, we considered our military families and their children to be great assets to our schools, but we, nevertheless, wanted to supplement our revenue as the law provided. I handled the significant amount of paperwork associated with the program and Thad took care of the Ft. Rucker and Washington involvement and lobbying.

We were strongly encouraged to attend the annual national meeting of the organization in order to participate in the sessions about changes and concerns, as well as visit our legislators to lobby for continuation of the program. Thad told me he was going to the meeting and wanted me to go with him. Neither of us had ever been to DC, but both of us got a new Yancey Parker suit, dusted off our old ones and packed up to fly to the Washington meeting. I had flown only once in my life, unless you add the trips on my Uncle Tommy's crop-duster. We arrived at the Washington National Airport with zero experience dealing with exiting or getting luggage or hailing cabs there. We finally got a taxi, threw our luggage in the trunk, and jumped in. As the driver pulled off, he asked us, "Where to?"

We gave him the name of our hotel. He quickly pulled to the curb and said, "You guys got to get out; this is a city cab. You need a DC taxi." We dragged our luggage to the curb, dodging other autos all the while and finally got us another taxi to DC.

We got to our room late after being unnecessarily driven around and conned by our driver for a 20 dollar fare. (It was a six-dollar fare for the reverse route when we went back to the airport. Oh, well, country boys go to town.)

Our trip got even more interesting in the late evening as Thad began to unpack his luggage and put his clothes in the closet and drawers. After a good while passed, he began to let out a string of expletives as only Thad could, so I asked, "What's wrong?"

He responded with gritted teeth, "I left my damn shirts!"

"You what?"

"I left my shirts at the damn house!" At the time I was a little smaller than now and he was a little larger, so a loaner was out of the question. After some more wailing and gnashing of teeth, we set out on foot looking for a store to buy a white dress shirt. The only place Thad found was in the back of a drug store. When we got back to the room, Thad grudgingly displayed a white, see-through nylon, sorta dress shirt out of the 50's era. "This is all I could find and I'll wear it 'til I get another one tomorrow and you better not say a damn word." I assure you I had no intention of saying anything.

Thad, fully embarrassed, attended his first Impact Aid National Meeting, wearing his "new" nylon shirt. (Incidentally, after years of involvement, Thad went on to become national president of the organization.)

During the early period of his Superintendency, Thad was as combative as he had been as a football coach. It wasn't that unusual early on for him to consider every call from a disgruntled parent about what another child said to their child on the playground as a personal insult that he was ready to go to war over. The same response came when a football player's dad called to lodge a complaint about insufficient playing time, etc., etc., etc.

One of my jobs early on was to help talk him off the ledge before fisticuffs ensued. Thad's name for me gradually changed from "Word Man" to "Conscience." We would normally discuss such issues and he would say "I damn shore ain't gonna do that."

Often at the end of the day, he would shout from his office, "Bad Gladys, get me a cup of coffee and get Conscience a diet coke." Then he would shout, "Conscience, come in here." When I got into his office, he would usually say something like "Okay, Conscience, I'm gonna talk nice to him but that loud mouth better not start anything." Over time, Thad got a little milder in regard to such instances and it was seldom necessary for me to "talk him off the ledge."

Eventually, there was hardly a day that Thad and I didn't end with a diet coke, coffee, and discussion of events, issues, plans and responses as we moved forward along with our beloved Enterprise City Schools. As we had these sessions, we grew closer and closer to the point that we also talked about personal issues from time to time.

As we became more and more open with each other, we also became more and more honest and respectful of each other and I grew to love Thad like a daddy. Although he wasn't that much older than me, he became a father figure to an old Samson boy whose father had abandoned him and his mother shortly after his birth.

I think Thad liked our relationship but sometimes considered it a weakness on his part. More than once, he told me after one of these sessions, "Conscience, I ain't never gonna get this close to another one."

After 10 years of growing with and learning from Thad, I reluctantly thought it was time to move on professionally if I were ever going to do so. He hesitantly agreed. I finally, with mixed feelings, took a Superintendency in another school system. Freddie and I and our two children cried all the way from Enterprise to Jasper and we always hoped to work our way back home.

Thad and I maintained our great relationship even after my leaving Enterprise. In fact, shortly after I moved to north Alabama, one day after work, Thad drove alone from Enterprise to Jasper to attend my first school board meeting as Superintendent. He had called my school board chairman about attending but I had no idea that he would be there.

I was shaking like a leaf as my first Board meeting began, even before realizing that Thad was in the audience. After being recognized by the Board chairman, he ragged me up and down before ending with one comment that I'll never forget. He said, "Ladies and Gentlemen, you got a good 'un." He then presented me with a plaque of appreciation from him on behalf of the Enterprise School System and walked out and drove back to Enterprise.

Many years later, when our son Bryan contracted leukemia, Thad called me one or two times a week to check on him and to pray for him and Freddie and me.

Freddie and I used to visit Thad and Janice, his bright and beautiful wife, periodically after he retired, to check on his health and talk about the "good ole days." The last time I saw him, I told him I appreciated all he had done for me. Out of awkwardness, I sheepishly said, "I love you like a daddy." We shook hands and sorta hugged, I said goodbye to Janice in the next room and as I went out the door, he mumbled, "I love you too, Conscience."

FINAL THOUGHTS

When Freddie, our children and I had the good fortune to work our way back to Enterprise via Dr. Joe Talmadge and the Enterprise State Community College, we developed a lot of new friends and acquaintances but Thad was always there. When I ran for mayor, Thad was a major mover in the process. Those friends from the college as well as those in City Government, as well as the new leaders in the Enterprise City Schools, including Bob Phares who took my place as Assistant Superintendent, became great friends and supporters but it is not within the scope of this to expand on those as much as I would like.

I dedicate these loving memories of Thad to his beautiful, bright, and devoted wife Janice, his son Bill, and his beloved deceased daughter Bitsy. I also thank all those who assisted Thad's family in caring for him as his health declined. I particularly thank and commend Mart and Bob Tomberlin for their devoted assistance to Janice in Thad's care. I am sure there are others who deserve such recognition of whom I'm unaware. May God bless you all.

Thad and Tim Alford

Bob Phares

I am so very thankful to my longtime friend and cohort, Dr. Jim Reese, for giving me the opportunity to join with many others in remembering and honoring Thadius William Morgan,whom I hereafter will refer to lovingly as "Thad." The time I spent with both Jimbo and Thad will be cherished for the remainder of my life. I will never be able to put into words (and probably shouldn't) what time and challenging times we shared over the years.

My first encounter with Thad came by way of a telephone conversation at a time I was living in Starkville, Mississippi and serving as a fledgling principal at Starkville High School, a fine school located in a university community. The first call to Thad came as the result of my having been informed by a friend of a vacancy in the assistant superintendent's post which had come about as a result of the departure of Dr. Tim Alford who had been appointed Superintendent of the Jasper, Alabama City Schools.

Interestingly, and as time validated, the friend who had informed me of the job opening said to me prior to the call "Now Thad's a crusty ol' rascal, but don't let that throw you - his 'bark' isn't nearly as fearsome as his heart is BIG."

Upon hearing my friend's description and preparing an interesting conversation, I called Thad and sure enough I found him to be, well, let me just say...all business. His sweet, tender demeanor over the telephone reminded me of a number of the tough old coaches I had been around for much of my life. Sweet and tender???

A week or so later, I was invited to visit with Thad for what wound up being the first of three rather lengthy and intense interviews. Some might have perceived these visits as "shake downs" if not interrogations, but to be honest, I kind of enjoyed them. At the end of each interview, Thad would say to me, "Shugga Boy, you sure don't know much," which I could've told him in the first place. Had it not been for such heartening encouragement, I might at this point have begun to think that Thad was at least remotely interested in me for the job although he surely had not tipped his hand.

I remember saying to Thad as I was about to depart after interview #3 that if I was not to be chosen for the assistant superintendent's position. I would very much like to work for him at some point in the future. His response was "You wouldn't be working *for* me, you'd be working *with* me." Without a doubt this made an impression on me and confirmed my thinking that Thad was unlike some other superintendents I had known.

Soon after my third trip to Enterprise and another visit to Thad's lair, I received a call from him letting me know that he would be visiting my school (Starkville High School) on the following morning. Certainly I was pleased to know that he'd be paying me a visit, but I felt it necessary to remind him that I had only told my superintendent and assistant principals of my interest in a job with another school in another state.

At the time I was enjoying an amicable relationship with our faculty, staff, and most of all, some of the finest young people on God's green earth, and I did not in any way want them to feel that I was unhappy with anything about them or their school.

But wouldn't you know it, by the time Thad left that day, every teacher, every student, every custodian in the school knew what was up. Thad later told me that before leaving to go home he canvassed numerous and varied corners of the city asking folks what kind of school I "ran."

My thoughts about this particular day were simply, "Well, at least he hasn't gone through my closet...yet!" By the grace of the good Lord, as it turned out, no one appeared to me to have hard feelings toward me and for the most part wished me well. I was appointed Assistant Superintendent for the Enterprise City School at the March school board meeting in 1984.

Thad was never one to mince words. Most who knew him didn't really think of him as being profane, and yet he was a master at using plain language. One of the phrases he used quite often was "I'm gonna put it out there where the goats can get it," and another, when he wanted to kick it up a notch was "I'll make it plain as a goat's ass goin' up a hill." He had a real knack for taking the mundane and making it colorful, if not at times a bit more vivid than some really wanted to envision.

I remember once being invited to sit in with Thad for an informal meeting with Mrs. Ruth Harris who at the time was serving as President of the School Board and who had known Thad for most if not all of his life. She knew Thad well. Mrs. Harris was and is as fine an individual and as fine a board member as we have ever had.

Like Thad, Mrs. Ruth loved the schools fiercely and on this particular day which was just after schools had convened for the fall, she simply wanted to "talk school." This meant that she wanted to know what kind of school opening we'd had, how finances were looking, what we were expecting for the upcoming football season, etc. As the conversation went along, I noticed Thad getting more and more intense and before we knew it, Thad had kicked into third gear and started using some of the colorful wording I just alluded to.

By this time Mrs. Ruth had joined me in simply being quiet and listening....that is until she finally looked straight at Thad and said, "Hush, Thad, you're cussin' too much!"

I knew Thad had been a master teacher and coach when he responded by looking straight at me and said, "Boy, did you hear that?" The tone and timbre of the meeting quickly returned to its original state, and the meeting concluded with smiles. It was by way of this experience, this "lesson," that I learned to watch my mouth.

A number of years later I was enjoying a good visit with another of the schools' icons, Mr. Benjamin Franklin "B.F." Garth, known by many as "Prof." Mr. Garth had served for many years as the Principal of Coppinville High School and later as Principal of Coppinville Jr. High School. Prof was small in stature but great of heart, like Thad. The ever-present twinkle in his eye always reflected Godly wisdom and goodness.

It was during our visit on that day that I gained even greater insight into the life, heart, and character of Thad Morgan by way of another who knew him very well. In his soft, well-spoken manner, Mr. Garth said of Thad, "He's the only person

I've ever known who would sit up into the wee hours of the night searching for the "truth." Mr. Garth had a keen eye for goodness.

While it wasn't the first time I had been asked to join in one of Thad's" set-tos" with a principal, it was certainly one of the most memorable ones. It seemed that the particular principal had fallen short of Thad's expectations with regard to the operation of "his school." For those who knew Thad, you knew that he relied heavily on the principals and although showing it unique ways, he loved them – sometimes with tough love.

During the course of this particular morning's meeting, Thad began to gnaw on him like "ugly on an ape." Finally, as the principal's head hung low and his eyes were on the verge of tears, Thad told him, "Now get back over to your school and do your job; you're not a storekeeper - you're a school principal."

Needless to say the principal quickly got off the hot seat and high-tailed it back to the school. After a few minutes of silence, Thad turned to me and said, "Wait until after lunch and go see about him." Thad was a teacher and knew how to use the sharp stick of truth to bring about good results. He also knew human nature and could tell when kinder, gentler verbiage could also bring about the results he expected.

Those who knew Thad and the love he had for his daughter "Bitsy" also understood the special place he had for others who, for lack of better wording, were disabled or handicapped or needy. He knew them and loved them all as God's children. Not only did he understand their needs, he saw their unique abilities and oftentimes celebrated them.

I'll never forget the time when Thad and I were in my home-town of Birmingham for a meeting when after its conclusion he suggested that we drive out to the neighborhood where I had been reared. I had gone to Banks High School which was located on the next block over from where my family had lived. I had a hunch that seeing the school was the real reason for his wanting to take the side trip to south East Lake in the first place. After all the neighborhood where ol' Bob had cut his teeth had never been on anyone's list of "places to visit."

As it turned out, there was another motive for Thad want-ing to venture out to my former stomping grounds. He had remembered my sharing memories of my childhood buddy, Bobra. Bobra and her family had lived two doors down from us and was a very special friend, and Thad knew why. Bobra had suffered brain injuries at birth and although in some ways she was limited, she never allowed those limitations to keep her from playing waffle ball, kickball, making potholders, or drawing with me any time I wanted. Bobra was my friend and Thad wanted to meet her.

In typical Thad fashion, we pulled into the driveway of the house where Bobra lived with her mother and sister; then, even though unexpected, we were invited into the house for a visit. Sadly we found Bobra lying in a hospital bed nearing her life's end. Our visit that day was a brief one, but I will forever believe that somehow Thad knew he was needed then and there. It could have been a "God Thing" – the kind that only the Almighty can bring to fruition. Bobra, Thad, and I held hands as Thad prayed a prayer that no one, and I mean no one other than one very close to the heart of God Himself could've prayed. Thad was a man of faith if ever I have known one.

From my earliest days with Thad I could sense that he was different — different from anyone I had ever known. Without my knowing how long we might me together, I knew that someday our time would come to an end. Thankfully, while he was still with us, I shared with my friend the following on April 23, 2004. With there being no doubt that he possessed far greater command of the written word than I could ever hope for, for me these lines capture the life and legacy of Thad wonderfully well:

> This is the true joy in life, the being used for a purpose recognized by yourself as a mighty one; the being a force of nature instead of a feverish, selfish little clod of ailments and grievances complaining that the world will devote itself to making you happy.

> I want to be thoroughly used up when I die, for the harder I work the more I live. I rejoice in life for its own sake. Life is no "brief candle" to me. It's sort of a splendid torch which I have got hold of for the moment, and I want to make it burn as brightly as possible before handing it on to future generations.

> From George Bernard Shaw's *Man and Superman*

Thanks for the memories, Thad, and most of all thanks to Janice for sharing this crusty old rascal with so many for so long. You were the only one on earth who Thad really answered to. But wait...Janice had a counterpart, — Gladys Welch, Thad's longtime secretary. Gladys, by day, served as Thad's "handler" while Janice served as Thad's fulltime "keeper " and the love of his life. Thanks to both of these fine ladies.

Thad and Bob Phares

L – R: Calvin Garth, Janice Morgan, Thad Morgan, Gladys Welch

Bob Tomberlin

In the mid to late 80s while I was Principal of EJHS, I was offered an elementary principal's position in Andalusia, Alabama. I had to go over to the Central Office and tell Mr. Morgan that I was going to take the elementary position in Andalusia. When I told him, he said, "Damn son, I didn't know you wanted an elementary position."

My answer was that I had experience in the high school and the junior high school, but I had no elementary experience and thought it might be beneficial. At that point, he pushed back in his chair and looked up at the ceiling and said, "If you want to be an elementary principal, I'll give you an elementary principal's job here in Enterprise."

I said, "You don't have a position open, and I cannot do that." Thad stood up behind his desk and I was sitting on one of those old chairs that went to the floor and he said, "Son, don't piss in my ear and call it rain!"

I responded, "What do you mean?"

Thad said, "You will take an elementary principal's job in Andalusia, but you won't take one here in Enterprise?"

My answer to him was to give me a day to think about it and I'd get back to him. The next day I went over to see him and told him I had decided to stay at EJHS.

Thad's reply to me was, "That's a damn good choice, son."

I didn't leave EJHS until Thad moved me to the Superintendent's office in 1991.

In June of 1991, the position of Director of Operations for ECS came open. I was working at EJHS on a Sunday afternoon and Mr. Morgan came by, stopped, and came in to talk with me. He asked if I had time to go riding around and check schools out. He did that every weekend. When I got into the car, he told me that he wanted me to consider the Director of Operations job at Central Office. We rode around several schools and he told me about his plans to build a new transportation facility for our school system and he wanted me to be a part of that. We rode around and looked at every school and he shared the future plans he had for each one of them.

As we turned onto College St. headed back to EJHS, he asked me what I thought. I told him I did not know and wanted to think about it. As we pulled up to the front of the school and I started to get out, he asked me again to tell him what I thought. My answer was that I had a great faculty, great students, plenty of money in my general fund, and I thought I would just stay at EJHS.

I started to get out of the car and he said, "Son, I'm going to move your ass over there anyway." I spent twenty great years at the Central Office working with Mr. Morgan, Dr. Reese, and a portion of a year with Dr. Milner. The best years of my career were spent with Enterprise City Schools.

In October 2019 Thad had an extensive cancer surgery at UAB Hospital in Birmingham to remove his right ear. Janice, Bill, and I spent 18 hours in a waiting room after delivering Thad for surgery at 5 am. His surgery was a 12 hour surgery and we were taken back to see him briefly at 11 pm. Honestly, he looked dead. Janice and I could barely stand up after looking at him. He didn't know us.

We went to our hotel rooms and slept only a little while. We were up and back over to the hospital around 6 a.m. because we didn't know which floor or room he was in, and we expected to find him in terrible shape. After getting our information, we approached the nurse's desk and asked where we could find Thad Morgan. A lovely tall black nurse, Patricia, heard us and said, "Is this Janice? Lordy, we are so glad she's here! That's all he's asked about – where is Janice?"

We went to his room and he looked so much better than he did when we left him the night before. He had nothing to say to me, but he wanted Janice to come as close to him as she could. He had a catheter and he wanted it out! He told Janice to tell those nurses to take that catheter out. We sought the help of our sweet friend Patricia. The catheter was removed and Mr. Morgan was told that he could not get up by himself to relieve himself. He was to call for help.

Patricia had already figured Thad out. She took the urinal cup with her to the nurse's station. After a while Thad asked to get up and relieve himself. I went to get Patricia and she brought the tiny little white charge nurse with her to help her stand Thad up by the bed. Janice and I left the room.

Outside the door, we heard Patricia explaining to him that he would need help with the urinal cup. He let them help him stand up by the bed and then yelled, "LEAVE! I don't need help!"

The little white nurse ran out of the room – he scared her to death.

Patricia sauntered out of the room with her head bobbing, "He don't need no help..." She had just cleared the door when we heard the urinal cup hit the floor and Thad yelled, "HELP!!" I cannot explain the look on Patricia's face as she turned and went back into the battlefield.

From 2011 to early 2023 we shared Friday nights or Saturday nights with Thad and Janice. These two precious friends became part of the family – along with Bill. We've had many good meals in one of the little rooms in the back of McLin's Restaurant in Daleville. It always took us 10 minutes to get to the room because so many people stopped Thad to tell him how much he meant to them or if he remembered tearing up their behinds. He remembered them all and could say something personal to them that made their eyes light up. He loved them. They were his reason for getting up for many years of his life.

We've celebrated birthdays and anniversaries together. Thad, Janice and Bill shared Thanksgiving with us and our family. He would start asking me in December if they were going to be invited to Thanksgiving for the following year. He loved having a captive audience as he told his "old stories" during and after the meal. He never failed to remind Julianne Tomberlin Sneckenberger that she parked in his parking place ONE TIME but never again. And, Thad loved Janice. So much. Thad Morgan loved his "people" - that's for sure. But Thad loved Janice. He loved Bitsy and Bill. More than once he told me they had sacrificed for him, and he was thankful. There's a hole in our lives where Thad used to be. We are thankful for every memory of our one of a kind friend.

L-R Marcia Tomberlin, Bob Tomberlin, Thad Morgan, Janice Morgan

Brenda Weakley

Thad Morgan

Thad Morgan, that man.

Thad Morgan, that dear curmudgeon of a man.

If one wanted to define who he was it would be nearly impossible. For you see, he was the enigma that left you challenging your sanity. He was that man who made you examine every thought you had and defy you to argue. He loved to shock. He loved to shake you out of your complacency and demanded concise explanation as you sought to defend or justify the stance you had taken.

It is hard, even to this moment, to speak those words that each of us has locked in our hearts. It is hard to speak of the loss each of us felt when that call came. It is hard to know that the gravelly voice cannot be heard. Each of us has tales to tell that would make a stranger swear we had taken off in flights of imagination or at least traveled in a sort of dimension that could not be real. Yet each of us knows that he was as real as he could be. You could take him or leave him and he did not give a hoot.

BUT (notice all caps) the one thing he demanded was loyalty. It was a loyalty that was born out of his faith in youth and what he expected. You could disagree. You could seethe in frustration. You could argue 'til the cows came home, but be loyal to one common idea – that you do what was expected of you.

Did I dare to tell you that you could argue? From the first time I met the man, we stayed in one continuous argument. I was the bane of his existence. As he interviewed me in the EHS office (he had not become Superintendent but not moved to the Central Office yet) he became highly exasperated because I had informed him that I would not paddle a student. He grabbed up my references from my previous school, asked why did everyone say that I had excellent discipline and not waiting for an answer to Mr. Thompson and said that I would be his problem? I left his office not sure that I had been hired.

Jump ahead 10 years...same song different verse. Principal's position, "Would I follow policy of using paddling as discipline?"

"No, I will not."

Later, after being told I would become Rucker Boulevard Elementary School Principal and being there for some time, that man called me over to the Central Office, brought me into his office, shut the door, took his seat and asked, " Why didn't you lie?"

Befuddled, I said, "I beg your pardon."

Answer, "No, I could not tell you that I would do something that I knew I would not." Silence. Long drawn out silence. Head shake.

"You are a fool."

"Yes, I know."

Time went on, and I was back at the Central Office. Arguing with that man continued along with threats of dismissal. But you see, I had to represent the elementary program and elementary teachers and principals because everyone else was secondary. Raining, standing on the sidewalk, arguing had continued from inside. That man's frustration hit an all time high. "I am going to fire you tomorrow. You have gone too far. I will notify the Board in the morning."

Answer, "Yes sir, I understand. I know you will do what you need to do." A car pulls up giving me time to escape to my car. Sat for a few minutes thinking about how much I respected and loved him.

I was not fired. I probably deserved to be fired for being too outspoken.

Jump ahead one more time. Call to come to his office. That man gets up from his desk. I held on to the doorknob to make a quick exit. That man speaks.

"You know that everyone thinks we hate each other." They don't know that we love each other.

That last sentence speaks to my heart. I do so love that man.

I am sorry that I am not sharing so many things – for example the water pistol fight where I ended up with that man throwing a pitcher of water on me when I only shot one tiny squirt of water after he told me not to dare shoot him. How can anyone pass up a dare like that I ask you?

Sherri Royals

What can I say about Thad Morgan? Who am I kidding? He was ALWAYS Mr. Morgan to me. Yes, he was gruff and quite intimidating, but he likely had a heart of gold. One day when I taught 5th grade, I went over to visit Mrs. DeRamus who was in charge of our closet for needy students. I had a child whose father had been tragically killed in an auto accident. The mother had three young children and had also been quite severely injured in the accident. Thankfully, she was home with her children but could not work, and their car was totaled. Insurance claims were being processed, but in the meantime the family was in dire need of basic necessities and money to pay utilities.

Mr. Morgan stuck his head in Mrs. DeRamus's door and said, "Royals, why are you over here bothering us?" (If he liked you, he always greeted you in that manner). I relayed the story to him and before I could finish, he told me that he had heard about that accident but wasn't aware of the great needs. He went to his office and wrote a quite large personal check and told me to take care of their immediate needs.

He then said, "Don't tell anyone about this until I die" and laughed.

So, Mr. Morgan, I'm still following your instructions.

Hinton Johns

It's a pleasure to be asked to honor Mr. Morgan. Mr. Morgan held a special place in my life. I remember going to my interview with him for the position of Assistant Principal at Enterprise High School. He was extremely direct and let me know if hired it would be my job to get discipline right, and that I'd be in charge of getting the job done.

I got the job and found that he always "had my back," and in that position that knowledge allowed me to do the job as I saw fit. Even though the disciplinary job was not the most desired in the system, I thoroughly enjoyed my time in the position and getting to know the school personnel. As part of that, I feel I developed a close relationship to Mr. Morgan and he became Thad to me.

I suppose I got the discipline "right" enough that I was offered the job as Principal of Enterprise Junior High School. Again, he supported me and trusted me to run that school. He'd call with questions if he didn't understand a situation, but I knew I'd have his support even if he may have handled it differently. To an administrator, that is all you can ask.

I enjoyed working for Thad. He was a unique individual who deeply cared about his students, teachers, and support personnel. He treated all of us as his family, and that meant he could sometimes give a good tongue lashing or laugh with you at a situation. I was so lucky to have been able to work for him.

After retirement he'd call every so often, and we'd have gab situations about what was happening in the schools or remembering our shared past. Cheryl knew to get to the phone to me even if I was asleep because I always wanted to hear from him, and I valued his knowledge and take on things. I knew I was one of the lucky ones to be able to continue hearing from him.

From this it's easy to see I admired Thad and appreciated his sharing his knowledge with me about how to handle situations. He was stern and demanding but also had a sense of humor (sometimes at my expense). I miss him and know there'll never be another like him.

Oveta Carey

The first time I met Mr. Morgan was in July of 1991 during an interview for the principalship at Harrand Creek Elementary. On the next visit, Mr. Morgan informed me that we would ride around Enterprise so that I could see all of the schools. I was excited because I had heard so many good things about the Enterprise School System.

During our ride, Mr. Morgan gave me a history lesson of the school system dating back to the 1970s. The personality, clichés, and mannerisms of the previous school superintendent, Mr. Royce Snellgrove, were shared with candor, humor, and play-by-play enthusiasm. Mr. Morgan did not skip a beat with details of the meeting to announce school desegregation. He further elaborated on his relationship with Mr. Alfred Peavy. Their bond ushered in a spirit of friendship and unity.

All of this rich history was intriguing because Mr. Morgan added his own flavor and colorful language to each story, scene, and situation. Even now those stories are vividly recorded in my mind because Mr. Morgan repeated them with the same passion throughout the years.

The ride of the tour of the schools was even more eventful as we zigzagged across Enterprise. Mr. Morgan was driving like he was a bona fide NASCAR driver. It was when we crossed a railroad track and my head hit the ceiling of the car that I knew Mr. Morgan was no ordinary person. I tried to act calm and professional but every part of me was soaking wet with sweat or something. When we finally drove back to the parking lot at the central office, he happened to mention that he had once driven his car into the porch of a nearby house. When I got out of the car, I was speechless and had to steady myself. Once I recovered from the roller coaster ride through the City of Progress, I enjoyed hearing more Thad Morgan stories.

Another memory of Mr. Morgan was in the 1990s when the Enterprise Wildcats played the Dothan Tigers at Rip Hewes Stadium. Since I grew up in Dothan and graduated from Dothan High School, I thought I'd sit on Dothan's side with my mother. My mother asked, "Who is that man walking back and forth; is he the coach?"

I responded with a chuckle, "He's not the coach, but he's my boss."

Well...what do you know...the following Monday I spoke with Mr. Morgan about the game. After I mentioned to Mr. Morgan that I sat on Dothan High's side at a football game with Enterprise, he informed me that my paycheck was signed by Enterprise and that I had better sit my blankety blank on the Wildcat side from now on.

"Yes, sir." Case closed.

Since that time when I go to an Enterprise vs Dothan football game, I sit nowhere else but on the Wildcat side. Mr. Morgan left an indelible mark!

Those who knew him will always remember his seemingly gruff demeanor, legendary stories, but most of all his big heart.

He was a fierce leader who ensured that the needs of children were met. Those who served under his leadership understood his philosophy well and followed his lead. His love for Enterprise City Schools was unquestionable and unwavering.

There are many experiences with Mr. Morgan that will long be remembered. When I think of him, I smile. He put in the time that God gave him. He lived his life with purpose and passion. We often say that God broke the mold with Mr. Morgan. Perhaps that is what made him unique and a legend in his own time.

I am thankful that God allowed him to pass our way.

RIP, Mr. Thad Morgan

Cheryl Johns

I met Mr. Morgan when I was 27 serving on an accreditation team at the high school. Everyone on that team had glowing reports and only positive observations to report except me. I was there for Special Education and I was in a quandary because the reviews completed by the teachers were very poor except for themselves. I really didn't understand how excellent teachers could be operating such a poor program, as shown by their review. I talked with administrators and the teachers and really didn't know how to proceed so I was advised to speak with Mr. Morgan who had just been named Superintendent.

Mr. Morgan let me know it was my job to be honest and complete a report based on their reviews. He was very, very clear about this and I was totally taken aback at his directness. I went home that evening and explained to Hinton that I'd met Mr. Morgan and I understood his intent, but I'd never had anyone speak so plainly to me.

Hinton laughed and said, "Oh, he's crazy. That's just how he is."

I did exactly what Mr. Morgan said and gave the only report with many recommendations. Some were major. I knew he wanted to know what needed to improve that department.

I was then hired 13 years later. One of the things I learned as a member of a group on a trip to Andalusia to see a computer based program was to never intentionally get into a car driven by Mr. Morgan. I think I closed my eyes in fear several times! He really drove like a maniac!

Another memory is when I scheduled an appointment with him to discuss putting in reading programs in the junior high schools because I knew we had students who could not read well enough to pass the graduation exam; therefore, they would not be able to graduate. I knew in order to convince him to add these programs, I had to show how the programs would improve the lives of the students. I've worked in several systems, and I really never felt that I must above all show how the students would benefit. To me, this was Mr. Morgan's strength. He cared first about the students and everything we did must benefit them.

Another area of my job, Section 504 Coordinator, had me in three hearings with lawyers and stenographers. Even though I was always apprehensive and nervous, I was never nervous about Mr. Morgan's support. We had a plan with the intent to benefit disabled students not in Special Education, and we followed that plan. I appreciated he didn't ask questions and allowed us to defend them. I think most superintendents would have settled instead of going to a hearing. We won those hearings.

I appreciated Mr. Morgan. I felt secure in making decisions related to my job, and I knew I would be supported. That's rare in most systems. I appreciated him for that.

Superintendents, Principals,
and Other Administrators

David Carter

This first story is about the first time I ever saw Thad Morgan. Not being from Enterprise, I had never heard of him. In 1970 when I interviewed for a job as VIE (Vocational Industrial Education) Coordinator and VICA (Vocational Industrial Clubs of America) Advisor, Charles Howell was the Principal of Enterprise High School. After our interview he walked me over to Superintendent Royce Snellgrove's office.

When we walked in, two men were arguing in rather loud voices. I asked what was going on, and Mr. Howell told me it was only Mr. Snellgrove and Coach Morgan discussing a situation. I asked if he always spoke to the Superintendent in this way, and Mr. Howell said, "Oh, it's OK. They've known each other since Thad was a baby." I wondered if I could ever work with someone who would speak to his boss like that. Little did I know that Thad would be my boss from 1974-2001.

I was Assistant Principal under Thad from 1974-1979. I usually arrived at school before him, and one morning he called the office to say he would be late. I asked if everything was OK, and he gruffly let me know it wasn't. He had gone out to get into his vehicle, only to find tires removed and replaced with cement blocks. He also said he suspected who the culprits were and wanted to see five male students in his office as soon as Janice could get him to school.

When he arrived, he was in furious Thad mode. He got the

boys into his office behind closed doors, and all kinds of yelling and shouting were heard. He demanded a few other students be sent down, many coming in saying, "I didn't do anything!" After hearing what he thought was the truth, he took the guilty to his house and made them remove the blocks and replace the tires. He came back to school with the boys plus one cement block which he used as a platform to administer the "bend over punishment" he thought appropriate for the prank!

Thad was a well-known presence on the sidelines of Wildcat football games. At one game he was really making his presence known, yelling at officials and causing them concern. They complained, and the head official called to the press box demanding to speak to the Principal. When I spoke to the official, he said a citizen on the sidelines was creating a disturbance and needed to be removed or our team would be penalized. I listened to the complaint and then explained that the so-called "citizen" was my boss and the Superintendent of Education. I could not and would not TELL him to leave. I did call down to the field and asked an assistant coach to try and get Thad to calm down or we would get a penalty. Only when Thad realized he might jeopardize the game did he stop harassing the officials.

When Thad was interviewing coaches to replace Coach Paul Terry in 1974, one assistant coach was a well-known coach from Montgomery. Thad always liked to "take a ride" when he wanted a serious conversation so he got the coach in the front seat and told me to sit in the back and listen to the interview. He also pulled out a big plug of tobacco and shared it with the coach. At every stop sign both front doors would open, and

Thad and the coach would lean out and spit.

The coach interrupted Thad several times, and Thad finally told him to shut up and listen as he explained what he wanted in a high school coach. The coach continued to interrupt and repeatedly called Thad "Tad." After the third time, Thad told him, "If you call me Tad one more time, I'll kick your butt out of this car." Needless to say, this coach did not get the job!

Those of us who knew Thad well remember his caring and compassionate side which was not often shown. My brother passed away in 1996 and was to be buried at Arlington. Thad happened to be in Washington, D.C. at the same time he was attending Federal Impact Aid funding meetings. He had to arrange transportation because Arlington is outside the city, but he left important meetings to attend my brother's graveside service. I have never forgotten this kindness and sacrifice. Thad could be stern and demanding, but there was never a doubt that he cared deeply for his friends and colleagues. I always knew he had my back in every situation.

Aaron Milner

THAD MORGAN AKA "THE CHAMELEON"
(WHO ALSO LOOKED OUT FOR THOSE LESS FORTUNATE)

My career in education is deeply rooted in the Enterprise City School System where I had the great fortune of attending as a student in the 1980s and serving as teacher in the 1990s before branching out to serve as an administrator in the system beginning in 2001. Each of these life/career events was heavily influenced by the leadership of Mr. Thad Morgan during his tenure as Superintendent of Education.

When reflecting on my time as a student, Mr. Morgan's wife Janice (Mrs. Morgan) who served as an English teacher at Enterprise Junior High School and Enterprise High School looked out for me throughout those formative years. I am quick to point to her as a role model for me as an educator. The care she demonstrated to me as a very average student may have opened the door for Mr. Morgan to accept the recommendation of Coach Bacon and Mr. Carter to hire me as a teacher and coach at Enterprise High School.

During my time as a teacher and administrator in the Enterprise City Schools, I constantly observed my colleagues and frankly was in a bit of awe. I was surrounded by men and women who were outstanding educators and school leaders. However, there was no doubt who was driving the culture in which students felt valued and loved regardless of their circumstances in life where teachers knew they were supported when holding students accountable, and a culture that demanded administrators lead their schools. I once heard Mr. Morgan say, "Never be a shopkeeper as a school leader – lead every facet of your school – don't just open the door and sit in the office."

Every employee knew the level of high expectation set and modeled from the leader at the top. Excellence can easily be taken for granted when it is the norm, and when success abounds, individuals outside a school system often fail to recognize the sacrifice, pride, and decision-making required to ensures it continues.

Mr. Morgan and his leadership team refused to rest on their laurels. They treated Enterprise City Schools as a diamond they were always polishing. A rare culture to be found in any organization was evident each day within the school system. It was obvious Mr. Morgan cherished his role as Superintendent, and his leadership made Enterprise City Schools a key economic driver for the city of Enterprise.

Two examples of his leadership prowess come to mind when I think of Mr. Morgan. The first is a leadership trait that won't be found in a textbook but was a priceless experience to observe. I have often referred to Mr. Morgan as being a "chameleon" when it came to dealing with people. His ability to adapt to people and circumstances was one of the most important lessons I learned regarding being a strong leader.

I have never met someone like Mr. Morgan who could shake a person's hand, sit down, and quickly know the type of person he was talking to and the manner in which he should shape the conversation. He had the uncanny ability to assess people's socioeconomic level, level of education, temperament, etc...within seconds of meeting them.

This may be hard for some to believe if they had never witnessed one of these conversations. For example, when a farmer entered his office, Mr. Morgan went into a mode and level of language that immediately put that person at ease while also showing they would be treated with respect and dignity. When a colonel from Fort Rucker wanted to meet with him, I witnessed Mr. Morgan present a completely different demeanor reflective of the situation. At the end, even if they agreed to disagree, parents he met with knew he had the best interest of their child in mind.

Yes, I would argue he treated people differently, but he never wavered on his integrity in treating students and parents the same in regard to board policy and supporting the child's teacher. Although he may have been chameleon-like when adapting to people, he remained steadfast in his refusal to negotiate or compromise on an issue that would bring his integrity into question. I wish I could have had the opportunity to witness these conversations more often than I did at that point of my career. His interactions provided a veritable clinic on communication skills and no-fear leadership, and those lessons continue to impact my current leadership style.

The second example of his leadership was not revealed to me until I became Superintendent of Enterprise City Schools. On a Saturday, immediately after being named Superintendent, I began perusing through the files in the Superintendent's office. Dr. Jim Reese was another mentor of mine, and I can assure you, if you ever met with him, he kept copious notes. I reviewed file upon file to ensure I was aware of the history and current state of the system. Dr. Reese also saved all of Mr. Morgan's files, many of which were more than a decade old. Out of intrigue I began sifting through those files.

To my surprise I discovered Mr. Morgan often made decisions that would be frowned upon today. However, I found it courageous and an example of his commitment to servant leadership. Multiple files were related to a lunchroom worker, an instructional aide, a custodian. Obviously, these are the lowest paying jobs in a school system yet some of the most vital roles in ensuring students are educated in a great environment.

Within those folders were handwritten notes that provided insight into this former superintendent. The documentation belied the hard exterior portrayed in Mr. Morgan's public persona and instead revealed a softer side reserved only for those truly in need. Notes such as "Ms. Jane Doe – child had emergency surgery – told her I would front her paycheck for the next month, and she could make payments in the following manner..." Another read, "Mr. John Doe – car is not working and cannot get to work – provided $500.00 and he will pay back by end of school year." Each employee initialed or signed the note, and I am confident they fulfilled their financial debt to the school system in addition to their debt of gratitude. As I read through those many folders, I realized that the "chameleon" had fooled me again.

Many think of a gruff, tough and domineering leader when they hear the name of Thad Morgan. I think of a person who defined leadership through his care for the stakeholders of his school system and his desire to have an impact on those less fortunate. When assessing my commitment to students and employees of the school system I lead, I measure my actions against the gold standard of leadership, Mr. Thad Morgan.

Thank you to both Mr. and Mrs. Morgan for the influence you two have had on my life and for showing the stakeholders of Enterprise City Schools and the City of Enterprise the lasting legacy of effective leadership.

Greg Faught

Although I never worked with Thad Morgan, I was the last principal he recommended in 2001 and had the privilege to know him well during my time in Enterprise, Alabama. Mr. Morgan was a plain dealer whose straightforward and honest nature reminded me of my father. Having the opportunity to contribute to these memories is a profound honor. I hope that you enjoy a glimpse into my memory of him. He was truly one of a kind!

In the spring of 1998, my fiancé, Helen Brown, an Enterprise High School graduate, knew she had me on the hook and wanted us to reside in Enterprise, Alabama. Helen arranged a meeting with Mr. David Carter who was still serving as a long-time Principal at EHS. After briefly meeting with Mr. Carter, he introduced me to Dr. Bob Phares who was Assistant Superintendent at the time. A short talk later, Dr. Phares escorted us through the lobby of the central office to meet the Superintendent, Mr. Thad Morgan.

Upon arrival, Mr. Morgan stood up and greeted Helen and asked about each one of her family members. He invited us to sit upon a couch across from his desk. This was no ordinary couch. It was tan in color and when we sat down, we sank to floor level, like bugs. He literally talked down to us from his desk. It was a surreal feeling to be sitting in the Superintendent's office because where I was from, no one actually meets the Superintendent.

Nevertheless, there we were, sitting in front of a man wearing a blue-striped short sleeved button-down shirt and a pair of slacks. Mr. Morgan was also chewing tobacco, and I remember thinking THIS IS WILD! When he finished his short chat with Helen, he looked down at me and in a gravelly voice asked, "What do you want?"

After replying that I wanted a job, he asked a few questions and said that he might have something for me and to report back for an interview with him and Dr. Reese on Friday. When I asked about the position I would be interviewing for, he told it was none of my damn business. I felt my heart sink while wondering what the hell I was getting myself into! He advised me not to wear a coat and tie but to dress comfortably – that I was only visiting Helen's family for the weekend and likely had no dress clothes. As it turned out, the opportunity which happened to be for an elementary principal's position, did not work out for me.

However, three years later in 2001 I was recommended to him by Dr. Reese (Incoming Superintendent) to be the Principal at Enterprise Junior High School. Mr. Morgan had planned his retirement for the end of June, and it had already been decided that Dr. Reese would be the next superintendent. The only reason I know that I was the last principal Mr. Morgan recommended is because he forgot to do it during his final regular board meeting.

Back in those days a dinner would be held after the board meetings, and while everyone was in line to prepare their plates of food, one of the board members asked Mr. Morgan who the next principal at EJHS would be. Realizing that he forgot to handle that part of the agenda, he reconvened the board meeting and made the recommendation formal. When I asked him about that later, he said, "Now you know how much I think about you."

When it was time to sign the contract, I met with Mr. Morgan and other central office staff inside a "lions' den" of spectators, some for a laugh and others just out of curiosity. Mr. Morgan was ready to put on a show.

After briefly reviewing the contract, Mr. Morgan said, "We are paying you too much damn money." That remark drew raucous laughter from everyone and made my blood pressure shoot through the roof. I told him that I would be the best principal in the system, and he quickly told me that I wouldn't make the top 80. Feeling the need to prove my worth and save face, I pointed out there were only 10 principals in the system. He replied, "Exactly!" The gallery erupted in laughter again, and I turned red with embarrassment having been reduced to 81st at best. Had to start somewhere, I guessed. Shortly after the others went on their way and it was just Mr. Morgan and me in his office, he prepared to hammer out the details.

My hands were shaking when he told me to come behind his desk and sign the contract. As I knelt and tried to steady nerves, he pulled me close to him and said in a very low and affirming voice, "Greg, you're going to be great!" Luckily, he spared me and I began to realize what a unique individual he was.

One of the long-standing rituals in the Enterprise City Schools included a formal inspection by Mr. Bob Tomberlin and his staff to ensure that schools were ready to open. Principals back then would work hard to ensure the buildings and grounds were spotless and well-groomed for the big "walk through." After my first full summer as Principal in 2002, Bob Tomberlin pulled up in his truck and had Mr. Morgan with him. I remember thinking that despite our best efforts, we might get exposed and maybe even embarrassed during the inspection.

Mr. Morgan barreled out of the truck like being shot from a cannon and appeared ready to inflict damage. Even the freshly cut blades of grass stood at attention as if the old man was a drill sergeant – eager to pluck the bad apples from their platoon. As for me, I just tried to maintain my composure. The hay was in the barn at that point!

While still under the portico and before entering the school, Mr. Morgan stopped and asked me about Helen. Hoping to get a chuckle or soften the moment, I told him she was mean to me. I will never forget his response: "Good, I hope she beats you with a stick, works you like a dog and makes you sleep in the yard." Glad I was wearing dark blue dress pants that day because I briefly lost control of my bladder.

The inspection was brief, but Mr. Morgan took his role as "guest inspector" very seriously. With great care he scanned for dust as closely as a bride would for leg stubble on her wedding night. After several grunts and grumbles Mr. Morgan and Mr. Tomberlin left the school and barely said goodbye. A few days later Mr. Tomberlin came by and told me how impressed Mr. Morgan was with the cleanliness and readiness of the school. Of course, that made my day.

Mr. Morgan had impeccable timing when dealing with people. He could sense when a compliment was necessary or when a stiff jab might help keep us on our toes. One evening we were walking together into Hillcrest Elementary School for a Board Appreciation Dinner. He told me that he liked my suit, and I said "Thank You." He asked if Helen picked it out for me. I was amazed at the question since she had been with me during the purchase so I confirmed his suspicion. Mr. Morgan told me that Helen had great taste in clothing but piss poor taste in men.

I agreed!

Later that evening during a prayer before the meal, Mr. Morgan lost his balance and stepped awkwardly on my foot. In an attempt to lighten the situation and make him feel better, I admitted having large feet. Out of the side of his mouth he whispered, "Yes, but you have a small mind." I remember thinking that Mr. Morgan must really like me.

After his retirement when our high school football games were still played in *The Hole* (Bates Memorial Stadium), Mr. Morgan sat with current administrators on the visitors' side. I remember in great detail watching him stake out his spot one evening while wearing a lime green, short-sleeved button-down shirt. I thought here is my chance to get even so I complimented him on the shirt.

Sensing something was up, he looked out of the corner of his left eye and said, "Thanks. Maybe I'll let you wear it sometime."

I chuckled and said, "Oh no, Mr. Morgan, I don't want to wear that shirt. Does Janice (his wife) know that you have been in her closet?"

He picked up his aluminum lawn chair and tried to hit me with it. He called me a name and threatened to kill me. As he gathered his composure and continued setting up, I saw the curve of a grin on his face. He liked a little push back every now and then.

Oddly to some, taking shots and delivering insults were ways to endear himself to those he really liked. However, if Mr. Morgan ever had a sense that someone he cared about was going through an unfortunate event, he became a source of comfort. I saw it many times, not just with me but with others, and it always came from a good place in his heart. He was genuine and always wanted to know about my family and how everyone was doing. It wasn't just an extension of courtesy, he really wanted to know. In later years he shared many thoughts about his life and what he knew was eventually coming. In true form he was amazingly candid and didn't hold any punches when sharing with me.

During my time as Superintendent Mr. Morgan would frequent the office to see everyone and say hello. When I hadn't seen him in a while, I would call or stop by his home just to check in. Most of our visits were quick, but he was never shy about asking what my plans were or what approach to pressing issues would look like. He cared deeply about the school system and wanted the best.

On one occasion Mr. Morgan wanted to go for a ride. We left the Central Office in his pick-up truck and turned left on Alberta Street heading west. He became animated while talking at one point that he was turned sideways in his seat, shaking his finger and not watching the road. As we drifted into the other lane and into oncoming traffic, I calmly told him we were about to go head-on with another vehicle.

Without hesitation he quipped, "I bet we'll win" and abruptly swerved back into the right-hand lane. Scared the stuffing out of me! I always looked forward to seeing Mr. Morgan because it gave me an opportunity to ask questions and gain perspective about upcoming decisions I needed to make. I didn't always agree with his opinions, but there was value in everything he shared.

While Mr. Morgan could be rough around the edges and appear to be a tough nut, he was amazingly thoughtful. In a few instances I watched him balance his courage with great consideration of others. Many people misunderstood Mr. Morgan and didn't realize that his true strength lay within that delicate balance and his well-timed ability to communicate in the right way at the right time. Beneath the rugged exterior stood an extraordinary kind and compassionate soul who enriched the lives of those who had the great fortune to know him. I miss him dearly.

Rick Rainer

During the 23 years that I worked with the Enterprise City Schools, I have many fond memories of Thad Morgan, but one sticks out in particular.

First, Thad always, and I mean always, asked about my family, especially my four children. He had a love for children. Of all the things he was so good at, I believe his love of children is what made him such a good school man.

One day during the summer, the year eludes me, I had to bring my two youngest children to work with me. Not long before the end of the day, he called me at the high school and said he heard I had the kids with me and he wanted to see them. By the way, I was an Assistant Principal at EHS at the time so I walked across the way to the Central Office with Will and Leanne. When we walked into his office, he immediately told me to go away – that they didn't need me and to come back in 20-30 minutes to get them. Of course I did what he said and left with a bad feeling about it. Will was about 6 years old and Leanne was 3, and they could be a handful - especially Will.

In about 20 minutes I walked back over and as I passed by Gladys's desk, she was laughing and shaking her head. I went into the office and there were my two children standing on his desk jumping onto the couch that faced it (the one you sunk down into and had to look up at Thad). I had immediately started taking off my belt but was stopped in my tracks when Thad, who was laughing hard, said "Leave those children alone. I told them they could do it, and they have also been eating candy!"

He also made sure I was not to punish them when we got home. For the next several years every time the kids were at the school, they would ask if they could go jump off the desk again!

There are so many other stories, but this one I will never forget!

Ed Weeks

STOREKEEPER

Storekeeper is a title I'll always remember fondly that I got from Mr. Morgan. What does that title mean? Let me explain.

You see, I had the privilege of serving as a principal under Mr. Morgan's tenure. I was Principal of the beautiful College Street Elementary School from 1993-2005. During this time I developed a capacity to run what I liked to call CSESISD or College Street Elementary Independent School District. To say the least, this gave me many opportunities for a summons to the Superintendent' s office for let's just call it "counseling." Mr. Morgan once asked me if I even had a copy of the *School Board Policy Manual*. He suggested I find one and read it while reminding me that it is not the job of a principal to develop School Board Policy but to enforce already approved policies that I just might find in the suggested manual.

What I was supposed to do while on storekeeper status was simple. He said I was to do the following until he told me otherwise:

1. Go to the school every morning. Unlock the door.
2. Go into my office.
3. Sit at my desk and stay there and do nothing else.
4. At the end of the school day get up from my desk.
5. Lock the school door.

Of course, having to explain what was involved in my being Storekeeper at our principals' meetings to the other principals and/or at other gatherings where he had the opportunity to have me elaborate on my new job requirements was always "entertaining."

During the counseling sessions I had the opportunity to learn some pretty good sayings that once I heard them, I began to use them myself. Two of my favorites:

1. "Mr. Weeks, don't piss in my face and tell me it's raining!" I loved that one, and lots of principals heard that one too.
2. "Mr. Weeks, that's as plain as a goat's ass going up a hill."

Anyway, I loved working for Mr. Morgan. He expected you to do your job and trusted you to do it. He held you accountable and had counseling sessions with you when you did not meet his standards.

The most important thing – when he told you he loved you, he meant just that. As he liked to say, "We had a pretty good run." Indeed we did!

Brent Harrison

The following stories are a couple that stand out in my relationship and interactions with Mr. Morgan that transcended from my being a high school student, teacher, coach, assistant principal, and Principal of Enterprise High School.

The first time I ever remember meeting Mr. Morgan I was a summer worker at the bus shop on Carroll Street in 1991. My uncle Dennis Johnson was the Transportation Supervisor and was able to recommend me and my brother, Brad for jobs even though we lived and went to Dothan City Schools.

I was an 8th grader and vividly remember Mr. Morgan driving up the dirt parking lot in the back of Carroll Street in his brown Chevrolet Caprice...at a high rate of speed. The car came to sliding stop almost as if it was slammed in park before it ever came to a complete stop. Out from the driver side emerged Mr. Morgan.

I was washing a school bus along with Steven Kelly, Chris Johnson, Antonio McClain, and Keith Miley and as Mr. Morgan was walking by and he stopped and looked at me and growled.

After the growl, he asked, "Are you Johnson's nephew from Dothan?"

I responded with a "Yes sir."

He growled again and as he started to walk away, he said, "If the world needed an enema, they'd stick it in Dothan!"

I turned back to wash the bus and saw all the guys scrubbing furiously. Confused and insulted, I asked the other guys, "Who the hell was that?"

Simultaneously, they all answered, "Mr. Morgan – the Superintendent. Shut up and get to work!"

After moving to Enterprise and later working for the Enterprise City Schools, I learned that Mr. Morgan loved saying certain towns would be a great spot to insert an enema. Really, any towns other than Enterprise and Auburn were great spots/ towns to insert an enema.

By my senior year at Enterprise High School, I had spoken to and interacted with Mr. Morgan a lot. He was always a presence on the sidelines during football practices and at games. You always knew if he liked you because he would call you ugly names and give you the middle finger as he drove by in his Caprice.

One day in particular, I was leaving the Blue parking lot during lunch. I drove a red Jeep and had a couple of sophomores, Ben Bowden and a couple of others, who couldn't drive, riding with me to Cutts' Restaurant. I was stopped at the end of Blue awaiting to turn right towards Cutts' as Mr. Morgan's car was coming down the street. As he drove by, he had his right arm extended across the passenger seat and was shooting us the "bird." Amazingly, he had slowed down to ensure that we saw it, and I could even see the smile on his face as he drove by.

A few days later, Trent Thompson and I, who were office aides, were at the window of the front office as Mr. Morgan walked by. He was walking into Mr. Carter's office across the way and looked over at us with a scowled look on his face. Trent and I thought it would be funny to give Mr. Morgan the middle finger. He was about to open the door to Mr. Carter's office when we knocked on the glass. He turned around and we had our middle fingers pressed up on the glass and we were dying laughing. Mr. Morgan immediately busted out laughing and gave us the thumbs up.

Ten seconds later, he emerged from the office area with a paddle and pointed to ground for us to come out of the office. We came out of the office and had to face the glass window we were just behind and looked at Mrs. Rakestraw as Mr. Morgan proceeded to beat us. I'm not sure how many times we were paddled, but I'm pretty sure it went beyond the state approved "3 licks!" A few days later he walked by the front window again and waved at Trent and me with big grin on his face. We did not give him the one finger salute this time...

In 2005, I had returned to EHS as a teacher and coach. On the first day as a coach during summer workouts, I remember we had just returned to Coach Collins' office in the field house after running all of the players off. We had just sat down, and I was sitting on the floor beside Buck Hanson and Matt Rodgers who were sitting in the only chairs in the office. Coach Collins was going over the agenda for the rest of the week when the door leading outside to the hill slung open and Mr. Morgan busted in. Almost everyone said, "Hey, Mr. Morgan."

He didn't say a word and just scanned the entire room. He

scanned back to me and said, "Damn, you have gotten fat!" and immediately walked out without saying a word. As he went to shut the door, he looked back at me and smiled and shot a wink at me and shut the door. He was never one to say it was good to see you or glad you are back.

To me this was his way of saying, "Glad you are home."

Several years later, after I had been named Principal of Enterprise High, Mr. Morgan stopped by to see me. As an assistant principal at EHS, I saw Mr. Morgan stop in to speak to Matt Rodgers dozens and dozens of times. He never was one for appointments or asking if it was a good time to talk. It was always a good time to talk to him. The same was true for me.

It was my second day as Principal and there was about an hour and a half left in the day, and in came Mr. Morgan.

His first words were "They'll hire just about anyone these days, won't they?"

We shook hands and he told me how proud he was of me. We had a little small talk and Mr. Morgan gave me some advice.

He told me that "If the teachers don't like you, the students don't like you, and the parents don't like you – then you are doing a hell of a job!"

He went on to say that to do this job right, no one is going to like you. He then said that this job was the hardest job in the system – he had been the Principal and Superintendent and by far the high school principal position was the hardest one.

Mr. Morgan went on to say that the job was a heart attack waiting to happen and I needed to be prepared. He said my friend circle is about to become very small and that's okay. To do this job right, you probably shouldn't have a lot of friends – it will only make the job harder. He told me that I needed to find a release and the release needed to be routed in my family. It was by far the most profound advice I had ever gotten as an administrator. In truth, his advice has helped me make it through my career as a high school principal.

Ed.'s Note: In his entry Mr. Harrison mentioned Matt Rodgers. Matt was a beloved teacher, coach, asstistant principal and principal at EHS during the first 2 decades of the 21st century. He became the President of Enterprise State Community College in 2017. Matt died of cancer at age 50 on June 1, 2022, less than a year before Thad"s passing. Matt loved Thad, and Thad loved him. I know Matt would have had some great stories about Thad, but he left us way too soon.

Mike Cutchen

I only worked in the Enterprise School System for three years. There are many memories of the superintendent who gave me my first opportunity to be an elementary principal, my life-long dream. Whenever we visited he never failed to ask about my father and my children. He showed a genuine interest in the wellbeing of my family.

Mr. Morgan also made it perfectly clear that we as school administrators worked for the Board of Education and constantly reminded us of that when we spoke of our assigned school as "my school." He had a way of putting you in your place when you crossed one of the Central Office staff and would let you know that was the same thing as not obeying his authority.

It only happened once during my time in the system but some of my fellow principals experienced Mr. Morgan's wrath more frequently. Regardless of how many times you got in Mr. Morgan's dog house, you always knew he loved you and would do what he could to help you be a successful administrator.

During my tenure with the Enterprise School System I would exercise by walking for an hour every afternoon after I left school. On one of my walks which were in my neighborhood, I came upon the access to the Enterprise High School football complex. Looking for a change in scenery, I decided to go in and walk around the track. To my surprise I was not alone.

Mr. Morgan was also walking on the track.

Those who knew Mr. Morgan knew he was a very competitive person. I did not know this. It did not take me long find out, however. I was a pretty fast walker but as fast as I walked, Mr. Morgan would walk faster.

He eventually had a 10 yard lead on me, and then I realized that he was not going to let a younger man beat him at anything – even walking.

It was a difficult time for Mr. Morgan when I decided to retire in Alabama and take a job in Georgia. There were several other principal vacancies, and Mr. Morgan was concerned with hiring the best "suspects" he could for the jobs which was consuming a lot of his time. When I had not heard from him in a while which was unusual because he checked on all of us principals regularly, I went to see him and told him that I thought he was mad with me because he had not checked on me in a while.

He emphatically replied, "Hell no I am not mad at you. I have to find a replacement for you and several other people." Whenever we talked or met after I had moved to Georgia, he would remind me of that conversation. He also got pleasure by sharing it with others at gatherings of former employees of the Enterprise School System.

After moving to Georgia, Mr. Morgan came to see me twice, once when I was working in Seminole County and once when I was working in Coweta County. His pretense in coming to Seminole County was to meet my wife whom he did during lunchtime in the high school cafeteria. I really think he wanted to check on me and see how I was doing.

He came by to see me a second time in Coweta County on his way to see one of the "boys" who had played football for him when he was in Villa Rica. He told me his former player was having a difficult time, and he needed to check on him. I think he was checking on me also.

When we visited on the phone or in person, Mr. Morgan would tell me that I was one of the good ones that got away too early and reminded me that I was a good school man. It always made me feel proud that he felt that way. I will always be thankful for the opportunity he gave me and the time I worked under his leadership.

Angela Seals

THE SIGNATURE THAT IMPACTED AND CHANGED MY LIFE

Mr. Thadius Morgan was a part of my life for a number of years. On three separate occasions his signature changed the trajectory of my life.

The first time was when I was a student at Alabama State University. The time had come for me to do my student teaching, now referred to as an internship. My desire was to do my student teaching at my Alma mater, Enterprise High School. I was informed that I needed a form signed to get my permission to do so. The Superintendent at the time refused to give permission. His rationale was a student from Alabama State University had never conducted their student teaching in our system before.

My parents and advisor encouraged me to speak with the Principal, Mr.Thadius Morgan. I made an appointment and talked with Mr. Morgan. My form was signed after a few choice words about how this made no sense. Mr. Morgan not only signed my form. He also placed me with my former 10th grade Biology teacher, Mrs. Myrl Whittle.

The second time was after teaching for one year at Daleville High School; there were no openings in the Enterprise City Schools. I wanted desperately to teach in my hometown.

An opening became available, and I interviewed with the Principals of Enterprise Junior High School, Dauphin Junior High School, and the Superintendent Mr. Thadius Morgan. After the interview, I was called and a decision was made for me to teach at Dauphin Junior High School. My letter of offer was signed by Mr. Morgan. I accepted, was hired and taught at Dauphin Junior high School for 16 years.

My third experience was in Administration. Mr. Morgan encouraged me to pursue a certification in Administration. After teaching 10 years at Dauphin Junior High School, I received my certification from Troy State University. This certification blessed me to serve as a 10-month Assistant Principal at Northview High School in Dothan, Alabama for five and a half years. I was spending time early one morning when our phone rang. The call was from Enterprise City Schools. I was asked if I was available/interested in interviewing for several administrative positions.

I met with and talked with Dr. James Reese who had been appointed as Superintendent and Mr. Rick Rainer, the Principal of Enterprise High School at the time. We talked and I felt that the Assistant Principal position at Enterprise High School was a great fit for me.

I was asked to report to the Superintendent's office to sign my letter of acceptance. The man sitting behind the desk was Mr. Thadius Morgan. It was his last day as Superintendent. He had a letter of offer for the position of Assistant Principal at Enterprise High School. He made the signed offer and I accepted. All three of these signatures greatly impacted and changed my life forever,

Stan Sauls

My story begins at Enterprise High School in the summer of 1996. I'd recently graduated from Troy State University, and I was seeking a full-time position for the upcoming fall. At that time Rick Rainer, who was an assistant principal at Enterprise High School and who had coached teams that I had participated on at Elba High School in both football and baseball, gave me the opportunity to teach summer school at EHS. Toward the end of summer school, Coach Rainer asked me if I was interested in a full-time position for the fall at EHS; if so, I was to report to the office of David Carter, who was the Principal.

I had been offered several positions at other schools but teaching and coaching at Enterprise High School would be, as Disney so aptly phrases it, a dream come true. So, I anxiously awaited my end-of-day meeting with Principal Carter. Upon entering his office that afternoon, I was introduced to David Carter, Bill Bacon, and Thad Morgan, who was, without saying, extremely intimidating. Coach Bacon and Mr. Morgan expressed to me that they needed a teacher/coach for the upcoming year, but that it would more than likely only be for one year. Despite the limited time frame, I gladly accepted the position.

My first experience at Enterprise High School during the school year of 1996-1997 was invaluable. The coaching experience

I gained by working with the Enterprise High football staff was immeasurable. Also, in the spring of that year Coach Bill Bacon presented me with an unforeseen opportunity. Coach Bacon expressed that he and Thad Morgan had discussed starting a soccer program at EHS. I explained to Coach Bacon that since I was from Elba, Alabama, I knew more about ice hockey than I did soccer upon which he congratulated me on becoming the first soccer coach for EHS. Due to Coach Bacon and Mr. Morgan's belief in me and my ability to coach a sport about which I had no previous knowledge, I entered upon a surprisingly successful coaching career, eventually becoming the Head Soccer Coach at Dothan High, Head JV Soccer Coach at Prattville High, and once more Head Varsity Coach at Enterprise High.

I would be remiss if I did not mention the teachers of the EHS social studies department that took me under their wings, mentoring and assisting me as a classroom teacher. Brenda Stinson, Lee Bradley, and Kay Ciuzio quickly instilled in me that I was a teacher first and a coach second. During my career in education one of the positions that I am most proud of serving in is the instructor for advanced placement history at Enterprise High School, which is one of the most rigorous courses offered. This opportunity would have never occurred if not for the tutelage of these renowned teachers.

Through my professional journey, Thad Morgan was instrumental in supporting my educational endeavors, wherever they may have led me. He would go out of his way writing me letters of recommendation or making a personal phone call. In 1997, with his support, I was able to obtain a teaching/coaching position at Dothan High School. I taught history and coached football/basketball under Coach Jimmy Addison and Coach Jimmy Golden. Dothan High School had an extremely talented football team that season, and we had to meet Enterprise High in "the Hole." The Dothan Tigers won convincingly that night; and as I walked across the field shaking hands, Thad Morgan approached me with an emphatic, "You sons of bitches." I took that from Mr. Morgan as a job well done!

My educational career has taken me from Enterprise High, Dothan High School, Prattville High School, and back to Enterprise City Schools. I received my first opportunity to serve in administration in 2012 when Judy Thomas took a chance on me as the Assistant Principal at Old Junior. Mrs. Thomas and I eventually became the administrators at Dauphin Junior the year Enterprise Junior was closed. I later became an assistant principal at Enterprise High School when offered a position by Matt Rodgers. In 2020 I was given the honor of becoming the Principal of Enterprise High School. The year 2020 is a year that almost everyone would like to forget, but it is the year my dream came true.

The details of my professional journey may seem trivial, but they are in fact quite quintessential to the legacy of Thad Morgan. No matter how my career path twisted or turned, even when it took me straight to our rival, Mr. Morgan was with me every step of the way, offering his unique brand of mentorship and support. There were many times over the years that his coaches or administrators may not have liked what they heard from Mr. Morgan, but it was, in truth, always spot on and given because he cared.

Thad Morgan was never wary of an audience. His thoughts were given with a purpose, and that was to improve his beloved Enterprise City Schools. Even after he retired, his devotion to the continuation of excellence in our school system never wavered; he would often drop by to offer his memorable words of wisdom that would not only give a message but more often than not a good chuckle. On a couple occasions the staff personnel in the EHS office, not knowing the legacy of Thad Morgan, would quake in astonishment at his direct and often brash guidance. Despite their shock, my response to Mr. Morgan would always be, "Yes sir!"

Afterwards, to those who obviously did not know of Mr. Morgan, I would explain his long-time position and how influential he has been to Enterprise City Schools. I would explain that Enterprise City Schools would not be the system it is today without the fearless leadership of Thad Morgan, without the careful and compassionate advice cloaked in abrasive missives intended not to tear one down but actually to build one up to excel. Thanks to Mr. Morgan, not only has ECS excelled, but so have I.

Charlie Abernathy

In 1974 I was hired as a defensive football coach at my alma mater Enterprise High School. I had graduated from EHS in 1966. That same year Bill Bacon was hired as the Head Football Coach at the school. He had been coaching at B.C. Rains High School in Mobile. He moved here driving a worn-out Biscayne Chevy he used to move football equipment from place to place. He was using 2 x 4 to prop up the back of the front seat so only one person could sit in the back seat.

Billy Hildreth had a hunting camp up Highway 167, and he invited Coach Bacon and me to go on a deer drive; Billy said to ask Thad Morgan, the recently named Principal of EHS to go with us. Because it was an early morning deer drive, we left home while it was still dark. Coach Bacon picked me up first and then we went to pick up Coach Morgan. I got in the backseat.

We started up the highway and as the sun came up, Thad noticed something and said, "I can see the road! I can see the road! There's a hole in the floor, and I can see the road!"

Coach Bacon just smiled , and Thad said, "I'm riding in the backseat on the way home, and you're gonna ride up here, Abernathy."

I rode in the front seat on the way home.

After leaving, I became an EHS Assistant Principal and routinely handled all sorts of discipline problems. Coach Morgan was the Superintendent, and he told me when a parent wanted to see him about a student problem to let him know ahead of time so he could be prepared.

One time, however, there was an Army colonel who went to see Mr. Morgan when I didn't know about it in advance. At that time students had to have a pass, signed by their parents, to leave campus for lunch. The colonel's son started coming back to campus late from lunch. After the second time, by school rules, his pass was suspended until he'd been punished by either getting two licks or serving Saturday detention picking up trash on campus or being assigned some other tasks.

The male student said, "Nobody's going to give me licks!" Therefore, Saturday detention became his punishment. He did not show up on Saturday so that meant that if he left campus at lunch again, it was the same as skipping school.

On Monday he left school and when he came back without a proper pass to show to the parking lot monitors, the automatic penalty was a one-day suspension from school.

He was sent to the office, and I had him call his dad to come and get him. The colonel did that, then bypassed David Carter the Principal, and headed to Mr. Morgan's office. I did not know that until a few minutes later when I got a call to come to Mr. Morgan's office immediately.

Mr. Morgan repeated what the colonel had told him, and the colonel said to me, "You have exceeded your boundaries."

"No sir, he did not! Mr. Abernathy followed the book exactly! Your son and any other student will be treated the same way the next time he leaves campus without a pass. Colonel, you live at Fort Rucker which means your son can go to any school nearby, like Carroll or Daleville, but if he comes here he'll have to follow our rules. I support that."

The colonel was not happy with that decision and said, "Mr. Morgan, you are the most arrogant person I've ever tried to deal with!" He then stormed out the door.

"Thank you, Colonel. I thought I was losing my touch," Mr. Morgan said. Then he looked at me and said, "What are you sitting there for? Get back to work!"

That's what I did.

Coaches

Bill Bacon

In 1974 I was coaching at B.C. Rain High School in Mobile, Alabama. I was not looking for another job. One evening after I got home from football practice, I got a call from Coach Morgan who was Principal of Enterprise High School at the time. He asked me if I would be interested in coming to Enterprise to talk about the head football coaching job at the high school.

I actually didn't know where Enterprise was, and I certainly didn't know Coach Morgan. In fact I was not sure that this whole thing was not a prank by my coaches there at Rain High School. I asked him how he had gotten my name, and he less than politely told me that it was none of my (expletive) business how he gotten my name, and would I be interested in coming to Enterprise and talking about the job.

I decided that I was interested, and I polished my shoes and drove to Enterprise. In time I was offered the job. I took it and that started one of the best chapters in my life.

Coach Morgan liked to march up and down the sidelines during football games often shouting his opinions on what was happening on the field and correcting the officials' calls. One night one of the officials had heard enough and asked him if he was one of the coaches. He replied that no, he was just one of the bus drivers.

Coach Morgan was entertaining a lady who was not happy with something that was happening at the school. She went on and on starting each sentence with, "Now Dr. Morgan..." Finally he looked at her and said, "Madam, the only doctorate that I hold is a Doctor of Son-of −a-Bitchary."

Ed.'s Note: Coach Bacon was honored at EHS's first home football game on August 25, 2023 when the football field at Wildcat Stadium was named Bill Bacon Field. From 1974-2000 Coach Bacon's teams had a record of 210-85-1 with 2 State Championships, 2 other semi-final teams, and 17 playoff appearances. He is a member of the Alabama High School Athletic Association Hall of Fame and the Wiregrass Sports Hall of Fame.

Thad Morgan and Bill Bacon

James Daniel

Thad Morgan hired me as a teacher and coach when I was 21 years old. I was hired with no teaching or coaching experience. That was my start on a long journey. First step and Thad Morgan was an agent for me.

Coach Pat Dye, Head Football Coach at Auburn University , called to request an interview with me for an Assistant Coach's position at Auburn. Coach Dye talked with Mr. Morgan about me and what the salary would be for that position. When Coach Dye told him, Thad replied that I was making more than that in Enterprise. Coach Dye ended up hiring me, and Thad helped me get a raise before I ever started at Auburn. I give credit to Thad for that.

Ed.'s Note: James is one of the most humble people I have ever known. He was the first Black Assistant Football Coach at Enterprise High School. He coached at EHS from 1974-80, at Auburn University from 1981-1992, and in the NFL from 1993-2020. He coached on 2 Super Bowl Championship Teams. He is probably best known, however, for playing on an Enterprise Recreation League Men's Softball Team with several of us coaches and teachers in the Enterprise School System. Because of his lack of speed (just kidding, James) he was the catcher on that team.

Rex Bynum

It was the summer of 1991 and I was looking for a new coaching and teaching position. I contacted Cheryl and Hinton Johns to inquire about any openings in the Enterprise School System. My wife Kathy and I were high school classmates with Cheryl and Hinton when he was coaching in Opp. They informed me that there would be an opening as an assistant football coach and head baseball coach at Enterprise High School and that I should contact Bill Bacon about those two positions. I called Coach Bacon, and he told me to come to the field house for an informal talk and not a formal interview.

Coach and I talked for a while in his office and then he said, "Let's go up to the Central Office and visit with Mr. Morgan, the Superintendent." Now I knew a little about the reputation of Coach Morgan, but I had not met him so I was a bit apprehensive about this first encounter. I was dressed in coaching shorts and shirt so I was not exactly prepared to meet the head honcho.

If first impressions do tell a lot about someone, then I had the feeling Coach Morgan was not too impressed when he first saw me. As he and I talked, it seemed to me that he was skeptical about hiring me for the two openings. He told me that he and Coach Bacon would talk about what they wanted to do and that Coach would contact me the next day. Coach Bacon did call the next day and said that there had been a change in the open coaching position. He told me that Kevin Collins, the football coach at Enterprise Junior High was being transferred to the assistant football position at the high school and that his position was open. He wanted to know if I was interested in coaching at Old Junior. I told him no, and he told me if I changed my mind to get back with him.

Well, a former head coach Donnie Chesteen with whom I had worked gave me one of the best pieces of advice I ever received when I told him about the opening at EJHS and that I wasn't interested in going to a junior high. Donnie told me that going to the junior high would be a way to get my foot into the door in the Enterprise School System. I called Coach Bacon back and told him I had changed my mind and that I was interested in the open position. He told me to meet him at the school the next day and we would meet with the principal, Mr. Bob Tomberlin.

When I got to EJHS the next day, Hinton Johns was sitting behind the desk in the principal's office. I inquired about why he was there. He told me that he was the new principal, and this was his first day on the job! At that moment I felt that I was going to be the new Head Football Coach at EJHS! Hinton told me about the changes that had taken place in personnel and those changes had been approved at the school board meeting the previous night.

For those of you who are "old timers" in town you may remember these changes. Mr. Charles Howell retired as Transportation Supervisor for the school system, and Bob Tomberlin was transferred to his position; Hinton Johns was transferred from EHS Assistant Principal to EJHS Principal;

Assistant Football Coach Charlie Abernathy was transferred to Assistant Principal at EHS; and Kevin Collins was transferred to the coaching position at EHS. Thus, I got my foot in the door, and it was the best decision I ever made! I want to thank Mr. Morgan, Coach Bacon and Hinton Johns for bringing my family and me to Enterprise!

I did not have any more contact with Mr. Morgan until the first fall varsity football scrimmage that was held on a Friday night in Bates Memorial Stadium. Let me digress a bit to set the stage for this encounter. When official football practice began that season, the junior high coaches would be with the varsity in the mornings of two-a-day practices, and then we would have practice at the junior highs that afternoon.

Those of you who played football for Coach Bacon know that he ran a disciplined program to say the least! There were at least two paddles around the field house that were used by the coaches to administer justice to the players when it was needed. What always amazed me was the fact that when a player was called forth to be "set straight," he never protested and after the licks were administered, he always told the administrator "Thank you."

Well, let's get back to Mr. Morgan. I got to the field house early that evening and when I went in, I saw Mr. Morgan, Coach Collins, and Coach Hanson in the equipment room. I went in to see if I could help with anything in preparation for the scrimmage. While we were in the equipment room, the players were at their lockers getting dressed in their football gear. Mr. Morgan noticed a big offensive lineman named Tristan Nance at the first locker. Mr. Morgan bellowed out loudly and told Tristan to get into the equipment room "right now!"

Tristan had on his t-shirt and underwear because he had just begun to getting dressed. Mr. Morgan informed Tristan that he had whipped his daddy's ass, and he was going to whip his! Tristan had done nothing wrong, but he dutifully bent over without saying a word and received 2 licks with Mr. Morgan's ever present paddle. Tristan responded with the aforementioned "Thank you" and went back to getting dressed. I was absolutely amazed! The reputation that I had heard about Mr. Morgan was true.

My first football season at EJHS was surreal! That team was loaded with talent and was probably one of the best in the history of EJHS football. The team was loaded with talent. We ran the wishbone offense, and I had been coaching that offense for several years. The team recorded a perfect 7-0 season, and the only close game was a 14-0 win over Opp. The starting defensive unit coached by the veteran sage of coaches Woody Crawford gave up only one touchdown the entire season. The second unit gave up the other touchdown for a total of 14 points allowed for the season.

The first game that season was against our cross-town rivals Dauphin Jr. High School. The day following our win Mr. Morgan and Mr. Tomberlin came to our school to congratulate the team and coaches (the other coaches were Ed Weeks and Donnie Hand). We had t-shirts printed for all the players with the team motto on the back.

That motto was "WHO DAT SAY THEY GONE BEAT THESE CATS, NOBODY!"

After the season was over, I went over to the Central Office to invite Mr. Morgan to our football/cheerleader banquet (Martha Thompson was the cheerleader sponsor who had done a fantastic job). Gladys Welch, Mr. Morgan's secretary, was at her desk and the door to Mr. Morgan's office was open. He was on the phone but motioned me to come in. He was talking with a banker in town, and I could tell the conversation was not going well.

After he got off the phone, he told me that particular bank was not giving the school system the best rates for the system's CD rates. He told me that if he could make a dime more by moving the money to another bank, then that's what he would do. He told me he did his job to make the Enterprise City School System the best it could be and that he would always do that!

His final words to me that day were that he was picked by Mr. Snellgrove to be his replacement, and he wanted to do his very best to live up to Mr. Snellgrove's expectations. I told Mr. Morgan that the Enterprise School System had a superb reputation and that he was doing a masterful job! He told me that the people of Enterprise expect nothing less.

I forget the year, but we had another good football team at EJHS and had won the City Championship against Dauphin on a Thursday night. The next night the varsity team played a game at Bainbridge, Georgia. Mr. Morgan came up to me on the sideline that night and thanked me for not running up the score on DJHS the previous night. I told Mr. Morgan that I had been on the other side of those type games and made myself a promise that I would never do that to another team. He thanked me again for the job I was doing. That meant the world to me.

I did get called into Mr. Morgan's office during the time I was the EHS Baseball Coach. He did not "chew me out" but gave me some wise counseling. He didn't raise his voice and his language was not as "colorful" as it sometimes could be but I got his message loud and clear!

My wife Kathy was also fortunate to teach in the Enterprise School System. Our children Amanda and Derek graduated from EHS. Amanda is married to Lee Marshall who was a quarterback for the football team and pitched for me in my first season as baseball coach. Amanda's twins, Jackson and Kamryn just graduated from EHS. Amanda's youngest daughter Mary Kathryn will be a cheerleader for Dauphin Jr. High this season. Derek's son Whit is not old enough to attend school, but I know he will be a Wildcat! Once a Wildcat, always a Wildcat!

I would not have had the opportunity to submit these memories and information had it not been for Thad Morgan offering me a job with the Enterprise City Schools in 1991.

Marc Sieving

Coach Morgan was such a great man, and I am honored to be able to write about him for this project. One of the things I always admired about him was although he was a very busy man, he always seemed to make time to say hello to me and ask about my family. My first encounter with him was as a high school football player at Enterprise. He was a larger than life figure, and I had instant respect for him the first time I heard him tell Coach Bacon to be quiet. My eyes got so huge and I couldn't believe what I was hearing.

I loved hearing Coach Morgan talk to our team about how much he hated Dothan. He told us he wouldn't even buy gas in that town. He came into the locker room after we beat Dothan and told us how proud he was of us. That was awesome. He also referred to the players from Carroll High School as living in a town called Krazo when spelled backwards.

My father was on the school board, and I would get messages from the office to stop by to see Mr. Morgan. It was usually some papers that he wanted me to take to my dad. One day I got called down and went to see him. I had a big smile on my face and said hello as I walked into his office. He looked at me with the most disgusted look and told me to sit my butt down. My mood changed from happy to scared in the blink of an eye. He got on my tail because I had a bad grade in his wife's English class. He made me bring my grades to him every week to make sure that grade improved. Anything below a C, and I was going to get "tore up" by the paddle.

Looking back I'm very grateful he took an interest in me and got me right when I screwed up. My favorite memory of Coach happened years later when I was a football coach at Enterprise High School. We were playing Smith Station at home with the winner getting into the playoffs. We lost at the end of the game on a Hail Mary pass. I walked to the elevator and Mr. Morgan was on it. When I got on, he could see I was hurting for our team. He told me he loved me and gave me a big hug. That was one of the nicest things anyone has done for me, and I'll never forget it. He cared about Enterprise so much.

Ed. Note – Marc is currently the Head Football Coach at Elba High School.

Buck Hanson

As I entered the foyer of the Central Office of the Enterprise City School System on East Watts Street, I recall Ms. Gladys Welch welcoming me and attempting to prepare me for what was about to happen. I remember sitting in the foyer and hearing Coach Morgan talking to someone in a loud and heated conversation. As the person exited his office, I heard him yell, "Gladys, send him in." She looked at me with reassurance and said it would be okay.

When I walked in, he was sitting behind his desk. He pushed his glasses down on his nose and said, "So you want a job?" As I sat down on a brown leather couch, it appeared to sink into the floor as I began to sit. I looked up at him and said, "Yes sir, I do." I don't remember any X and O questions concerning football. He was much more concerned about his expectations of me in the school and community. I emphatically remember him saying, "Do your job to the best of your ability, and I'll stand at the door and defend you. You embarrass the school or community, I'll kick the door down." I believed him.

I remember as a student at Enterprises High School I went to use the phone one day. The office was rather full so I waited my turn. Coach Morgan was the Principal and was on the phone when he looked over and saw me. At that time he motioned for me to come into his office. While talking on the phone, he grabbed his paddle and motioned for me to turn around.

Doing as I was told, he gave me two good licks and sent me out. When I got back in line, he got off the phone and asked why I was still there? I told him I wasn't in trouble when I came up there. I just needed to use the phone. He thought I needed the licks anyway.

I'm not really proud of this story: My junior year at Troy University, we had a day off from practice. I decided to drive to Enterprise to watch the Cats practice. I got there early and was standing outside the field house waiting for the players to come out. Coach Morgan just happened to drive by and saw me. He stopped, said hello, and invited me to come to the field house. Inside the field house, he grabbed the paddle and said, "Sugar boy, don't you know you can't wear a Stroh's beer shirt around here? Here's a little reminder."

After a win, Coach Bacon would always ask Coach Morgan if he had anything to say to the team. Like clockwork, his exact words would be, "Damn good un boys!" That basically started the celebration because we knew we had made him proud.

When it comes to Coach Morgan, there are so many stories to share but many I can't repeat. I do know the love he had for this school and community. He would always ask about my mom and dad and my family as I got older. How he loved the Wildcats!! Seeing him on the sidelines and after games in the locker room will always be cherished by hundreds of fellow Wildcats. He had a unique way of showing how much he cared for you while he was either punishing you or verbally confronting you. When I think of Coach Morgan, I smile.

My wife Missy told me about a story that happened to her after she first met Coach Morgan. One afternoon, Missy was walking through the yard, heading across the street to the Central Office to apply for an elementary position. Coach Morgan, knowing her intentions, pulled into the parking lot, got out of his car, and yelled across the street. "Mrs. Hanson, just because your husband is a coach here, doesn't mean you'll get a job. Now, tell me what you're walking over here for?" The rest is history.

Ed's Note. Buck told me a Thad Morgan story that he did not include in his recollections. At an EHS football game when Thad was Superintendent of Education and walking along the Enterprise sidelines during a game as he usually did, a father of a player yelled at him. The unhappy dad shouted, "HEY THAD, tell Bacon (the head coach) TO PLAY MY BOY! PLAY MY BOY!"

Thad stopped walking, turned to the man, and said, "I'll tell you your boy's problem...it started at conception."

Kevin Collins

I was a recent college graduate looking for my first job. I made the 4.5 hour drive from North Alabama to Enterprise to interview with Bob Tomberlin at Enterprise Junior High School. I left before 4:00 A.M. to make the interview. I pulled into town, stopped at Jim Harrelson's gas station, and changed into a suit in a restroom on the side of the building.

After the quick clothes change, I found my way to "Old Junior" to start the interview. Mr. Tomberlin interviewed me for three solid hours. After he had asked me every possible education question known to man, he said, "I'm going to take you over to talk to Coach Bacon." I knew the reputation of Enterprise football and of course Coach Bacon, but I had never met him.

He was cordial enough as we began to talk, but that soon transformed into him telling me to demonstrate proper offensive lineman stance in my suit. He had me going through stance and steps for a good 20 minutes only pausing long enough for me to tuck my tie inside my shirt – no time to discard the jacket, just time to keep putting my hand on the floor in his office and talk like I knew what an offensive lineman should do. The only one left for me to meet now was Superintendent Morgan.

Mr. Morgan escorted me into his office for the introduction. I thought going in "Is he Dr. Morgan, Superintendent Morgan, or what?" I found it a little hilarious to put eyes on him – he was sitting behind desk In his trademark suit with his right shoe off, scratching his sock foot on the side of his desk.

Mr. Tomberlin excused himself, and we were alone in the office. A long, pre-dawn drive, three hour interview, stance and demonstration – I was exhausted by the time I first met Mr. Morgan. His first words to me were very direct. "Mr. Collins, what do you want from Enterprise City Schools?"

In a mental, physical and emotional fog by now, I needed to close this interview strong so I blurted out, "I want your job!"

Without pause, and giving his signature look with his chin lowered where he's almost looking up at you, he goes, "Well, you can have the damn thing!" He did not seem impressed by my initiative.

We talked for a short time. Then he said he wanted to show me around the high school campus. We walked out of his office where he asked Gladys, his secretary, where his paddle was. A PADDLE? What kind of superintendent carries a paddle?

We exited through the back door of the Central Office, walked beside the Ag Shop, and turned the corner by the Driver Education building. We met a student in a hurry coming around the corner.

Whop! "Thank you Coach Morgan."

Did that kid just thank him for paddling him? And did he call him "Coach"?

We continued on toward the concrete slab that used to be

there behind the gym. A girl was coming out of the third hall door when Coach Morgan called her over.

"Turn around!" Whop! "Thank you, Coach Morgan."

Neither kid had done anything wrong. Does this guy paddle everyone he sees? He asked the girl as she walked away, "What you gonna tell your momma when you get home?"

"I'm going to tell Mama that you gave me a paddling today."

He said, "That's right! Tell her just like I used to beat her ass when she was in school here!"

Standing near the outside entrance to the boys' gym locker room was a Big Black Man. He was quite intimidating then, I could tell 20 years or so earlier he would have had everyone's attention. I figured no one would want to make him angry.

Coach Morgan said, "Come over here. I want to introduce you to an Assistant Principal. "This is Kevin Collins. Tell him who you are."

"I'm Alfred Peavy, Super Ni**er," said Coach Peavy without hesitation.

Anyone who knew Thad Morgan could tell a hundred stories. I still see his school car up that incline by the field house, sparks flying as he bottoms-out the undercarriage of the car because he refuses to slow down when taking that embankment. Or Friday nights when he would follow the ball and signal to us how far to go for a first down.

A lot of good memories.

Paul Curtis

I came to Enterprise in the summer of 1986 to be interviewed for the teaching/coaching position at Dauphin Jr. High School. I met with several people while on this interview. Coach Bill Bacon, the Head Football Coach and Athletic Director met with me and showed me around the athletic facilities. Mr. Charles Henderson, the Principal of Dauphin Jr. High, met with me and gave me a tour of the school.

I also met with assistant superintendents and other principals in the system. They all made a reference to Mr. Morgan, asking had I met with him, etc. I felt that all these interviews and introductions were going well, but I sensed that Mr. Morgan would have to be impressed if I were to be hired.

Then it came time for me to go in and meet with Mr. Morgan so I am led to the Superintendent's office. As I enter his office, he shows me the seat I am to sit in. As I sit, I begin to sink about two feet down in the chair so that I am looking up at him.

I also noticed that all the "King's Men" (the administrators I had met with) have followed me and have lined the room behind me. Mr. Morgan goes around the room and asks each one of them if they had a chance to talk with me and what was their impression. He asked them one by one and thankfully all responses were positive. Mr. Morgan then turns and looks at me, leans forward and peers at me over his glasses and asks, "ARE YOU WORTH A DAMN?"

I looked up at him in my sunken seated position and said, "YES SIR!" I instinctively knew that any other response would not be good. He then pushes this sheet of paper in front of me and with emphasis says, "Sign right here."

I knew because my Dad had been a Superintendent that all hiring is done by the School Board, but I realized Mr. Morgan had just hired me. He just had that aura about him and there was NO doubt who was in charge here. Surely his recommendation to the Board would just be a formality.

Mr. Morgan then leans back and calmly says, "Well, we have asked a lot of questions of you? Do you have any questions for us?"

I said, "No Sir, not really but I was curious as to what my salary will be."

He then springs forward in his seat and peers at me over his glasses and again with emphasis says,

"YOU SHOULD HAVE ASKED ME THAT BEFOE YOU SIGNED IT!"

That was one of the many lessons I learned from this man. As I look back, everything he told me was true — like the time I was getting anxious to advance in my profession, and he got wind of it and came to see me. I can still hear his words of encouragement. Later when those opportunities came and I left the system to advance, he came and reminded me that I was one of his. That compliment is something I have always cherished because of its source. Mr. Morgan was a true leader.

Kevin Killingsworth

My first meeting with Coach Morgan was the summer of 1991. I interviewed for a physical education/coach position at Dauphin Junior High School. After the interview with Mr. Perry Vickers, Principal and Coach Bill Bacon, Mr. Vickers replied, "You need to meet with Coach Morgan." Mr. Vickers also added "Don't be surprised if Coach Morgan uses a few words."

Coach Morgan then asked Mrs. Gladys, his secretary, to have us to report to his office. As we entered his office, I noticed two high wing back chairs in front of his desk with a couch in between. Mr. Vickers hurriedly sat in the far wing back chair. Coach Bacon then sat in the wing back chair next to the office door. I was only left to sit on the couch in between the wing back chairs. I noticed as I sat on the couch, I was sinking further and further down as I looked up at Coach Morgan. I quickly adjusted my posture to the couch edge.

The conversation began with Coach Morgan asking me, "Boy, you want this damn job?"

I quickly replied, "Yes sir. I do want this job." Then he called for Godzilla (i.e. Mrs. Gladys). Coach Morgan told her to draw up a contract and bring it back.

Coach Morgan then asked me "What will you do next week when Coach Mack Wood calls and offers you a job at Elba?"

I told him that I would reply "I'll tell him I already have a damn job!"

Coach Morgan then replied "I know damn right you will because if you don't, I'll sue the hell out of your ass!"

Then Godzilla brought the contract in and I was told to sign it.

With football season beginning soon, I quickly began coaching. As the season progressed, things were not going as I had envisioned for the ninth graders. One Tuesday after our eighth-grade game had been rained out, I stood by the field house waiting for the football players to be picked up by their parents. I looked over and saw Coach Morgan who pulled up to me in his Park Avenue Buick. He rolled the window down and said "Get your ass in my car."

I thought he was about to fire me for not winning games. I just knew my termination was coming as I walked around to his car. Then I got into his car and he told me, "Let me tell you one damn thing." Again, I just knew he was about to fire me. Then he said "I've been checking up on you and you are doing a good job. If you get down on yourself for not winning games, I'll get all over your ass!"

I listened intently and continued to say "Yes sir" to him.

He then added, "Now, you can get your ass out of my car."

As I closed the door, in typical Thad Morgan fashion he sped off.

To some people this comment might not have meant much,

but for me this instilled confidence in me that I was doing the right thing for these kids. This quick conversation did wonders for my confidence and I knew he was backing me regardless of the game wins and losses.

After leaving Enterprise City Schools and many years of administrative experience, I continued to talk with Coach Morgan. He was always forthcoming in sharing that he was proud of me. I learned a lot from him and knew the importance of loyalty. He taught me to support your people always and care for them as people also. This left a profound impression on me that I've relied upon in my personal and professional life.

At one time, Coach Morgan showed up at the Central Office of Coffee County Schools while I was a Central Office administrator to visit me and check on me. The Superintendent at the time was Mr. Terry Weeks who had not met Coach Morgan but was aware of him through his reputation. After speaking with Coach Morgan for a few moments, I asked him to meet Mr. Weeks. Coach Morgan, in true fashion, began telling Mr. Weeks how sorry I was and how he hated he had to work with me. As I listened to this exchange, I laughed as Coach Morgan continued to share in his serious, yet joking demeanor.

Some years later, when I became the Superintendent of Coffee County Schools, I looked out the window and saw Coach Morgan getting out of his Jeep. I quickly noticed his struggle as he approached the Central Office entrance. As I approached the office entrance, I met him at the front door and invited him to my office. I knew he was experiencing some health issues. When he came in, he always asked about my family. He shared again how proud he was of me in my professional career. This meant the world to me coming from him. Knowing his health was declining, I offered that I wanted to share what he had meant to me. I shared that he had taught me how to deal with issues and controversies. He then shared "Aww. you need to hush!"

I looked at him from behind my desk and said, "Damn it, you are going to listen to ME this time. I would not be where I am if it had not been for you."

This was an emotional exchange for both of us. I was afraid if I didn't take this opportunity to tell him, I might not have the chance again. I was glad that I did because I only saw him one more time after this exchange.

Rhett Harrelson

Growing up, I always heard stories about the grouchy, rough around the edges, always carrying his paddle principal that everyone feared and knew as Coach Morgan. This information mostly came from my family members who grew up in the Enterprise School System and found themselves in the principal's office quite often. However, as I was starting my professional career at 23 years old, I had an entirely different perspective.

It was the summer of 2017 when Dr. Reese and I visited Coach Morgan at his home in Tartan Pines. I had just been hired as the Head Basketball Coach at Enterprise High School. Dr. Reese and many others were helping me start the Hoopsters Club that helps fund our basketball program. One of the immediate needs for our program was to purchase a "shooting machine" that cost roughly $8,500 at the time. Dr. Reese and I felt that we needed to pay Coach Morgan a visit.

We showed up at his house, and Mrs. Janice Morgan let us into their home and took us back to Coach Morgan's room. At the time Coach Morgan was sick and was not in great health and was not moving around well. We made small talk and joked around for a few minutes and then Coach Morgan slowly got up out of his chair and made his way over to his desk. He sat down, looked at me very seriously, and said, "Tell me about this shooting machine."

I told him all about the shooting machine and how it would be beneficial to our program. I explained the different ways we could use the machine in practice, how individuals could become better shooters, and my plans moving forward for the program. Coach pulled out his checkbook and started writing. While writing, he was telling Dr. Reese and me about his coaching days and how much he enjoyed coaching, teaching, and mentoring young people.

The grouchy, rough around the edges principal that everyone feared handed me a check for $500.00 and told me how proud of me he was. It was a visit that I will never forget and one that I will always cherish.

Ed.'s Note: Mr. Morgan's and many others' donations for the purchase of the shooting machine contributed to outstanding results. Coach Harrelson led the 2020-21 EHS basketball team to a Runner-up in the State Tournament and the 2021-22 team to the State Championship – the first time in the history of the school either one of those accomplishments had occurred. On a personal note, our grandson Reese Dowling was a member of the championship team.

Who Was Thad Morgan?

Mark Fuller
(Attorney and Judge)

Who Was Thad Morgan?

Before one can answer the question, "Who was Thad Morgan?" one must first answer the question, "WHAT was Thad Morgan?" It is almost like describing a hurricane to someone who has never actually seen one or experienced it firsthand. For those who have, you know that it is awe inspiring at a distance, violent up close and absolutely beautiful once you are in the eye.

Such was Thad Morgan. I grew up the majority of my life in Enterprise as Mr. Morgan's neighbor, and my father was one of the few people with whom Mr. Morgan was close. The first Tuesday of every month was welcomed at dinner time by Mr. Morgan barging into our home (of course unannounced and without warning) and hollering, "Ken, it's time to go to the School Board meeting." Both men were gruff on the outside but would give you the shirt off their respective backs but would not want anyone to know they had. They were also fiercely loyal and protective of the Enterprise City School System.

One story about Mr. Morgan that comes to mind that best encompasses these qualities happened in 1998. At the time I was serving as District Attorney and was very involved in the Republican Party in Alabama. A friend who was a local government official asked me to ride with him to Montgomery for some reason which I can't recall at this time. My friend had ambitions and possibly wanted to succeed Terry Everett as U.S. Representative upon his retirement.

We had a successful trip to Montgomery and were talking about my friend's future political plans when my cell phone rang. It was my father calling, and I could tell that I was on his speaker phone. From the volume and the tone of the call I also knew that something bad had either happened or was about to. As long as I live I will never forget the first words that I heard my father say. "Do you know what that crazy son of a ***** friend of yours has done?*

After I was able to decipher that the alleged S** was the person I was riding with, I asked him what he had done. He told me that my friend had been alleging that the school system kept two sets of books and had a $10 million surplus, and the city wanted to get that money. Keep in mind that I was riding in the car with the person who wanted to get that money, and he and I were the only two people in the car.

When I was able, I finally got into the conversation and asked my father (and Mr. Morgan who was in the office with him) to hold on. I turned to my friend and asked him if he had actually accused Mr. Morgan of keeping two sets of books and that the city wanted $10 million from the school system.

Knowing Mr. Morgan, this would have been akin to attacking Mrs. Janice, if true. My friend confirmed that he had indeed accused the school system of keeping two sets of books, and the city needed the money to fund some projects. My exact words to him were, "You are making a career ending decision!"

His reply was, "Thad doesn't even have the support of his own School Board."

I pleaded with him that the city should not go forward with this and that the next City Council meeting would have to be held in the high school auditorium because of how many citizens would show up in support of Mr. Morgan and the school system. For those of you who are familiar with this incident you will remember that the City Council meeting was eventually moved to the auditorium at the old Enterprise High School.

When we got back to Enterprise from our trip to Montgomery, my friend dropped me off at the law office on Lee Street. When I walked into my father's office, I was met by my father and Mr. Morgan and had to face the wrath of the accusations as if I made them myself. The die was cast for a showdown between the city and Mr. Morgan and the school system.

This incident showed me the fierce protection that Mr. Morgan had for the Enterprise City School System. He was like the wall of a hurricane.

I have seen so many young people that Mr. Morgan literally took into his home, helped out with clothes, money or personal help that he would provide and never want it to be advertised. This is just what I know about. I feel certain that there are many, many others whom he helped and they may not have known where the help came from. Those are examples that reflect the "eye" of Hurricane Thad and the beauty of his heart. He was one of a kind, and I am blessed to have had a chance to know him, licks with the "board of education" and all!

Dale Stinnett
(Businessman)

BENEFACTOR

My air-conditioning company had a contract with the Lowndes County school system and ran into some difficulty with the general contractor that we could not get resolved. My son and I made an appointment with the Lowndes County Superintendent Dr. Johnny Covington to discuss the issue.

When we entered Dr. Covington's office, he greeted us warmly and said, "I believe you are from Enterprise. Is that right?" We affirmed we were. He responded, "I am too."

Then he asked if we knew a man named Thad Morgan. Since both Slade and I certainly could claim to know Thad, we happily told him that we were well acquainted with Mr. Morgan.

Dr. Covington then shared his Thad story with us. Johnny Covington, he revealed, was a young boy from a single-parent home, a boy gifted with very little athletic ability but pushed by a strong desire to do well in school. He became involved in several extracurricular clubs at EHS. In one of them, he was selected to represent the school in a state meeting. Somehow, Thad knew about this situation and called Johnny to his office "across the way." He told the teen that he was about to represent Enterprise High School when he went to the meeting and when he spoke. Thad encouraged him by telling him what a fine representative he was. He also bought him some clothing for the trip and gave him some pocket money.

As Johnny became older and even more involved, Thad continued to motivate him to excel and to represent his family, school, and community well. He also continued to provide him with whatever would help him along the way.

Johnny knew that his mother would not be able to buy a class ring for him so he never mentioned it to her. Miraculously, though, he received a senior ring fitted to his size, thanks to the largesse of Thad Morgan. As his senior year commenced, he also knew he could not afford to go on to college; he began to consider to what plans he might make for "after graduation." He did not know that Thad Morgan was calling various colleges on his behalf and ultimately was able to procure a scholarship that would enable Johnny Covington to get a college education and degree. When Thad told Johnny about the scholarship, he also told the young man to keep him informed about any needs he might have. Thad promised to help him.

Johnny went on to earn his doctorate in education and to become the superintendent of a school system, much like his mentor. He gave Thad Morgan credit for what he was able to accomplish, not just credit for clothing and a ring and pocket money, but for motivation and inspiration and watch-care.

We never discussed the problem with the contractor – it went away that day. His final words were, "God bless Thad Morgan. I was one of many – how many we will never know- whom he helped without anyone's knowing."

Ed.'s Note See Dr. Covington's tribute to Thad Morgan elsewhere in this book. It confirms what Mr. Stinnett so eloquently described.

Nicholas McQueen
(Physician)

Though I never had the privilege of having Thad Morgan as a coach, principal, or superintendent, he was still an ever present figure in the football locker room during the 2005, 2006, and 2007 seasons.

He typically saved his best pep talks for the Dothan game. The speech was always concluded with his famous quote, "If I had two properties, one in Dothan and one in Hell, I'd sell the property in Dothan and move to Hell."

He was one of a kind with a heart of gold beneath that gruff exterior. His impact will be felt for many generations.

Richard Pipkin
(YMCA Director)

What can you say? There will never be another person as unique as Mr. Thad Morgan. You always knew where you stood with Mr. Morgan. He served on the Enterprise YMCA Board of Directors Personnel Committee consisting of seven people who hired me in 1977. I'm very thankful that Mr. Morgan had confidence in me for hiring me. He supported my family as long as we worked hard and had an outstanding work ethic.

Mr. Morgan was blessed with a wonderful wife. Mrs. Janice and God have blessed me with Twyla too. Mr. Morgan believed strongly in God and family. He loved his school children and his staff by supporting them.

God bless Mr. Morgan's family. Mr. Morgan and Mrs. Janice have made a tremendous difference in the lives of many families in the Enterprise City School System, their church, and their community.

Billy Jones

I met Coach Morgan around 1965 at Coffee Springs High School where my uncle played football. They would practice at night because most of the players farmed during the day. When he was Assistant Coach and Assistant Principal at Enterprise High School, he invited me to go with him to his last coaching clinic in Tuscaloosa. I believe that was in 1973, and Coach Ben Baker went with us.

One of the things I will always remember is Mr. Morgan and Mr. Ken Fuller helped a family member out of a bad situation. Mr. Morgan was always helping young people who had made bad decisions to get on the right track.

On a lighter note I was leaving the school, and he asked me to ride with him. He was checking lunch permits. He would pull up to a car and ask students for their lunch permits. If they didn't have anything, he would say "See you at my office."

When he was Superintendent of Education, I would drop off calendars to the office staff. He would hear me talking to his secretary Gladys Welch and call me into his office, and we would talk for an hour or more.

When my parents died in an automobile accident in 2004, Thad called me from Jacksonville, Florida. We talked for 30 minutes or longer.

What a great man and friend he was to me!

Ben Bowden

Lion-hearted and lamb-like – that's the way I would describe Thad Morgan. It's hard to pinpoint what made him that way. Maybe he always had a gout in his foot and a bur in his underwear (that's what it often seemed like)! Or perhaps it was, at least in part, the pain he experienced in losing his parents in such a tragic way or having to walk through the loss of his daughter, Cornelia Ann "Bitsy" Morgan. Whatever contributed to the making of Thad Morgan, I'm convinced we don't have many men like him in our society anymore – and that's a loss for us and for society.

My dad Jimmy Bowden played football for Thad back in the late 1960s. He told me stories about how Thad Morgan along with Head Coach Paul Terry were some of the hardest coaches to play for mainly because they wanted the best out of their players. My dad knew that Thad Morgan wouldn't settle for mediocrity, nor should he. That's a lesson my dad passed on to me and now I'm passing on to my children.

Back in the 1990s, when I was a student at EHS, I thought Thad was the grumpiest man alive. He would often growl at my friends and me as he walked down the EHS hallway. My mom Karen Bowden, who was a special education teacher, told me of another side of That Morgan though. She said he was a jokester with a big heart. For example, one of her female students came from a rough background where she was exposed to a great deal of foul language. She often brought *these choice words to school* and would very *innocently* repeat them.

Therefore, my mom came up with a list of words she was not allowed to say. On a number of occasions when Mr. Morgan visited her classroom, before he left he would call this particular student over and say to her, "Tell me again, loudly, what are the words you CAN'T say?" Naturally, this student would loudly say every cuss word in the book! Mr. Morgan would give my mom a wink and a smile and be on his way.

He was a jokester, but he also had a big heart. And that was *especially shown* through the way he *frequently visited* and *cared for* the special needs children. A lot people didn't see that side of Thad. He loved those children and, to quote Mary Cannon, "made them feel as important as the starting quarterback on the football team." My mom and the Special Ed department in the Enterprise City Schools always had exactly what they needed – Thad made sure of that. He made them feel special, and for that, he was special.

I believe this is just a little fruit that came from knowing his Savior, Jesus Christ. He and I had several discussions about the gospel. I served as his associate pastor at First Baptist Church Enterprise from 2011-2015 and then as his pastor from 2015 until he died in March of 2023. We would converse about how there is no amount of good that one can do for his community or church that can ever earn him a place in heaven.

The gospel teaches that only through faith in Jesus and his finished work on the cross can someone be accepted by God. Because Thad Morgan believed the gospel, we can look back at this seemingly gruff and grumpy man, a man who was lion-hearted and lamb-like, a jokester with a big heart, and we can have gratitude to God for giving us such a man who did so much good for the Enterprise City Schools and thereby our beloved Enterprise community.

Facebook Posts Following
Thad Morgan's Death

Facebook Posts Following Thad Morgan's Death on March 12, 2023

From Memories of Enterprise, Alabama Facebook Group

RUSS HARRELSON – MAR. 12, 2023

This is a "Memories" page so I wanted to share a memory or two of Thad Morgan (Maybe some of you can too)...I knew him as Coach Morgan and he loved football and the Wildcats. The opening game of my junior year (1984) we played at Prattville and we were #1. I had only had my drivers license for about 2 months and was a 16 year old starting QB that had no idea what I was about to get into that night in Prattville. They popped us and I did not have a good game and threw a couple of interceptions and a fumble. We had a few fans yelling at me (don't yell negative things at kids, they can hear you) and a few boo birds. That Sunday morning there was an editorial in a paper that said (I still have it in my scrapbook) that said "Cats need QB and improvement on defense to compete for championship"...

Well, this little 16 year old was devastated...Monday morning as I walked in my 1st period class (Introduction to Business with Mrs. Farris – 4th hall) she said "Mr. Morgan wants to see you ASAP in his office"....I had a good relationship with Coach Morgan but I took the long way to his office while trying to figure out why I had been summoned to his office...I walked in his office and he gave me a couple of licks because he thought I should have been in his office a few minutes earlier...He grabbed his car keys and said "Let's go for a ride"....Once we got in his car he started talking to me about the game. He talked to me about that editorial. He talked to me about Enterprise Football. He told me he believed in me. Told me he loved me. He told me the community believed in me and not to let a few nut jobs in the community get me down (I know Coach Morgan and my dad talked with the sports editor of the Ledger after that editorial and that was the last time I was called out by the sports editor.

(Ha)....Anyway, that was 1984. That was 39 years ago. I remember it like yesterday. We drove through Hardees drive thru and he bought me a biscuit and drink and we went back to school. I had to grow up real quick that year and Coach taking the time to tell me he believed in me and loved me was a "kick" I needed (we won 9 in a row after that as a side note)....
By the way, when we got back to his office and he gave me another couple of licks for leaving school with him without a permission note from my parents. Loved him! Will see you one day soon, Coach!

Mitzi Hurt Bradford

Oh what a precious man. I got in trouble for holding hands with some boy and had to sit in his office one afternoon. When he got finished lecturing me, I had the nerve to tell him what I did was not as bad as him threatening my Aunt Mary Hickman with tossing her out of the second story window at Old Junior High School (she was the teacher).

RECOLLECTIONS OF THAD MORGAN
THE MAN WHO COULD MAKE GOD CUSS...AND LAUGH

ROB PAUL

The night after my dad died, Coach Morgan and Jimbo Reese showed up at the front door of my parents' house. Best I remember, Thad shook my hand. Told me he was sorry and asked "Where's Betsy?"

Fast forward 8 or 9 years later. I'm the pastor at FBC Elba, and the two Coffee County EHSs are playing basketball in 36330 [Enterprise]. I show up at the game, and Coach is at his spot by the door. "What are you doing here?" I tell him I'm the pastor at FBC Elba, and he says, "That's just a damn miracle!" I said, "Yes, Sir, Coach. It is."

CINDY DUNAWAY

Russ, I was in the 10th grade when my dad died. Coach Morgan came and got me out of class after I went to school. He hugged me, told me he loved me and he was there for me. I never had the privilege of meeting his paddle, but I think both of my brothers did. Loved Coach Morgan, worked with him on situations as a police officer, he was amazing to work with. He was always concerned with the safety and well being of the students.

KAREN HUDSON MILLER

Me and my twin brother Keith graduated in 1976. Keith and a few of his friends always missed school the first day of hunting season. Coach Morgan knew why they were not at school but he would still call the house and say to my Mother.... "Ms. Hudson...sure hate Keith is not feeling well today...tell him I will hopefully see him tomorrow and come by my office when he gets here." He always wanted to know how they did on opening day.

RON HOLT

There is an awful lot of people that could post an awful lot of memories on here about Coach Morgan. But as I mentioned to another friend, what made it so special is that just like writing thank you notes, each one is personal. He made them that way. I know I could probably post a thousand, but one sticks out to me and probably has lasted longer than any. My senior year (1975) we arguably had the best team in the state. But unfortunately, we took a season ending heart breaking loss to Dothan in the final game. They went on to finals. With only a couple of minutes remaining in the game, I got hit and suffered a hip pointer and what turned out to be torn cartilage in my knee. I walked off the field so my parents assumed I was OK and came back to Enterprise. I was sitting on the floor in the dressing room when Coach Morgan (at that time Principal Morgan) came and sat down next to me on the wet dirty floor. He calmly asked if I was OK. After a few consoling words he stood up, held out his hand, and said "Come on, let's go see about that knee." He put me in his car and took me to the emergency room in Dothan. He called my parents and told them that he had me and would bring me home when we were finished at ER. They must have told him that they would head to Dothan because he told them. "No need for that. He is one of my boys. I will take care of him." On the way back to Enterprise we talked a little about the game and a lot about everything else besides the game. As we were pulling into my driveway, his last comments were what meant the most and I still remember to this day. "Ronny, you can have all the talent in the world, have the most talented team in the world, and still lose the game. You can't control that. That is football. But it is the lessons that you learn and the character that you build from that loss that shape you and make you into the image you portray and the man you will become. That is life and you can control that."

PAT KELLY

Coach Morgan used to catch me in the hall and would ask me, "Kelly, how much do you weigh today?" I'd tell him and he'd answer, "That ain't enough. Come in my office." I'd get a couple of licks and he'd tell me I had better have gained 5 pounds the next time he asked or I had more coming! I sure wish he and his paddle were around to motivate me to lose a few pounds now! Also, my Dad worked with the Health Department and I knew all of the health inspectors. I always knew when any of the schools in the district had been written up for any violations because I would get a call to come to his office and get licks for the lunchroom violations. The infractions were always minor, but the licks sure felt major! My Dad had a ton of respect and love for Coach Morgan. He will be missed by many.

LEEANN CAPPS

I always thought I kept a low profile in high school since I never got called to Morgan's office. I had graduated 12 years earlier and just started working for *The Dothan Eagle*. (My previous reporting jobs I didn't interact with school officials). I don't remember what the story was about, but I had to go to the superintendent's office, introduced myself and we did the whole interview. At the end he asked if we were done and I said yes. He then leaned forward and said, "I bet you think I don't remember who you are." I leaned forward in my chair and said, "I hope to God you don't remember who I am!" Then we both burst out laughing.

He also commented to me that the difference between a prom and a class reunion - the alcohol is on the table at the class reunion.

What a great man who will be missed.

KIM GILLEY HAINES

As a 1976 graduate of EHS I have many wonderful memories of this legendary Enterprise man. One that I will never forget is when I was a senior and I had lost my wallet apparently in the parking lot of the school. Someone came to the class I was in one day and told me Mr. Morgan wanted to see me in his office! Now I can honestly tell you that I had never been called to the office. That was one LONG walk! When I got there Mr. Morgan was so kind and told me right away, "You are not in trouble!" As it turned out he had discovered a boy who was in possession of my wallet and before he went any further he wanted to make sure nothing was wrong and that I had in fact lost my wallet. He was always fair to all the students and looking out for all the students. He will be greatly missed.

PUG MONTGOMERY SCHWERTNER

The saying goes that you don't always remember what people do, but you always remember how they make you feel. Although Coach Morgan always brought on a certain amount of fear/respect, I always felt he cared. As some of you already expressed, he was there for our family too when my father passed away when my brother and I were in high school. He was a good man and will be missed by many. Prayers and condolences for his family.

RECOLLECTIONS OF THAD MORGAN
THE MAN WHO COULD MAKE GOD CUSS...AND LAUGH

Facebook Posts from Celebrate Enterprise Group

DIEON PATTON (3/13/2023

Enterprise lost a legendary man yesterday with the passing of That Morgan. I know generations of us here have vivid memories of Mr. Morgan. I have 2 very vivid memories of him. First was my sophomore year in Pensacola, Florida. We had traveled there for a football game and for a reason beyond our control we (The EHS Band) were unable to perform at halftime. I remember vividly Mr. Morgan escorting and shooing everyone off the field AFTER the game so the band could perform our halftime show.

My second and most vivid memory of Mr. Morgan was my senior year – also at a football game...in Bates...EHS vs. Prattville. Prattville had just taken the lead with 1:08 to go in the game. Several events made this so memorable. The band began playing the fight song as Coach Bill Bacon sent out Alan Evans to receive the kickoff. With his heels just outside the goal line Alan took off down the right hand side of the field....down our sideline...Mr. Morgan was standing at the 20...He ran beside the sideline yelling "Run Boo Boo Run! So loudly we could hear it in the drum section OVER US playing the fight song. He followed Alan all the way into the end zone.

He was all about us kids...never one to spare the paddle...even if it was just a smack of motivation. He was one of a kind and will sorely be missed.

RIP THAD MORGAN

CATHY THOMPSON *(3/14/2023)*

I too have many stories of Coach Morgan that showed his caring and love for students. I thought he especially cared for me (after his boys of course, that he went from junior to high school to continue with them), but he made us all feel that way. He once told my dad not to worry about me, that I would be fine since I was with Tim Thompson. And that certainly turned out to be the case. I will never forget him walking up the aisle at Sheila's funeral and seeing Tim crying. All those years after high school, the man was still a giant to Tim as he was and will remain. I pray students will have someone in their lives to help build their character, but there will never be another Coach.

ALEX STREYER *(3/14, 2023)*

There have been many stories and thoughts shared about Coach Thad Morgan in the past few days. And probably volumes more in the future. I'd like to share mine – a very short one but oh so powerful.

"You SISSY!"

(sorry – I can't type it with his vigor or the other few words that probably followed (haha). That may sound like an odd sentiment at this time but those who knew Coach UNDERSTAND IT. Till this day some 50 years later, it still serves as MOTIVATION! His way of saying, "You can do better, work harder, dig deeper, and give it your all...and more."

THANKS COACH!!!

I think that the saddest thing about Coach's passing is there will be generations of students who will not be able to experience and share his leadership, friendship, his love...his MOTIVATION.

AMANDA N JOE YOUNG 3/14/23

"The Lost Boys" of Thadius W. Morgan

They came in droves, year after year
Some were lost in terms of family,
Some were lost in terms of belonging.
And others were lost looking to find their way.
He took these boys and showed them the way.
He pushed them to the limit,
Showing them all they could be.
He was forever their compass
Showing them the way.
When those Friday night lights came on,
The Lost Boys would play.
They played for the game,
They played for the fans.
But most of all they played for the pride set in
their mentor's eyes.
As time passed by the Lost Boys went on,
Some became laborers,
Some became more.
And though they went on, they always knew,
They were the Boys of Thadius W. Morgan.
And because of that they were lost no more.|

-A.J. Young

Selected Passages from Perry Vickers'
Eulogy at Thad Morgan's Funeral

Perry Vickers

(Selected Passages from Eulogy for Thad Morgan March 15, 2023)

When Bill (Thad's son) called me and asked if would conduct this service, I immediately began thinking about my association with Thad and what he had meant to the school system and city of Enterprise. When I say school system, I am talking about everyone who worked for the system - the kids first and foremost and then maintenance staff, bus drivers, lunchroom personnel, teachers and administrators. Whatever you thought about Thad, never doubt his love for the Enterprise City School System and his love for the city of Enterprise.

Thad's mentor was Superintendent J.R. Snellgrove. Thad's ideas as to how to run a school system came a lot from working for Mr. Snellgrove. There aren't many of us left who also worked under Mr. Snellgrove - Dr. Reese, it may be just you and me. Mr. Snellgrove taught Thad that principals need to run the schools. The Superintendent was responsible for recommending the right principals. Principals were responsible for recommending the right teachers and support personnel.

One time Thad took a question to Mr. Snellgrove. Mr. Snellgrove thought that Thad should have known the answer to the question. Mr. Snellgrove let his glasses slip down on his nose, looked over them, and told Thad that he might have made a mistake in recommending Thad.

Thad's advice to us principals was, "If you can't handle that, I will find someone else who can." Both men meant every word!

One thing Thad did do was to let principals be principals, and he backed us. He expected us to support our teachers. If he thought that we were wrong, there would be a butt chewing unlike any other – but it would be in his office behind closed doors.

Thad was known for his driving skills. I can personally attest to his ability to make a car do things you would say it could never do. I had the experience of riding with him and Coach Bacon to Andalusia for a basketball game. Everything was going fine until they started talking about football. It was just outside of Opp when one of them brought up the passing game. Just over a river bridge Thad started a down and out pattern. Luckily, he caught himself before we ended up in the ditch. The bravest thing I ever did was to take the keys to the car and drive us home after the game that night.

Many people just thought that they really knew Thad. Those of us who were on his administrative staff had the ability to see sides of him that few saw. We got to see him through the good times and the sad times. One of the saddest times was when his daughter Bitsy died. Other times were when one of his former players or students came upon tough times or passed away. Surprising to me was his ability to keep up with his former players from Georgia, Coffee Springs, Enterprise Junior High, and EHS.

I always thought that Thad missed coaching. After his work

was over for the day, during football seasons, you could usually find him down by the practice field watching practice. Prior to the games he would be in the field house with the coaches and players. Just prior to the start of a game he would ease down to the home sidelines. If Thad thought that the officiating wasn't what it should be, he could get quite vocal.

That brings to mind Thad's unique ability to communicate and his command of the English language. He could express his thoughts in such a manner that one could definitely understand what he was trying to say. He could adjust his vocabulary to suit any occasion. He could especially adjust it if Mrs. Janice or Gladys (his secretary) was present. There was one thing you had to admire about him. He tried to treat everyone the same. He expected the teachers and principals to do the same.

During my 38 years in the Enterprise City School System I was fortunate enough to have several good mentors, but the greatest were David Carter and Thad Morgan. David was superb with building care and school maintenance, and Thad was the best with finance. When Thad was Principal of Enterprise High School he was able to get it back on a sound financial footing and did the same for the school system.

What you will not find on Facebook or anywhere else are stories concerning Thad and Janice's giving to the less fortunate children and families. Very few knew about it because they wanted it that way. There was a very special place in Thad's heart for special needs children.

There was an unwritten rule back then that if a club or activity went somewhere or did something that required a fee, no child was to be denied going or participating due to the inability to pay. When the Big Blue Band went to the Sun Bowl in Arizona, all 220 of them went.

Behind the gruff mannerisms of Thad beat a big heart. He and Janice helped children and friends not for any tribute but because they truly cared. You know the mark of a good man or woman is not the wealth they may have or the position they may hold. It is his or her kindness and love for others.

Thad Morgan and many others left a legacy to the Enterprise School System. It was all about children being first. It was a legacy that required discipline, fairness, pride and sound educational principles.

Final Personal Thoughts

How could a man whose parents were violently murdered, whose daughter would need special services for physical and mental health issues her entire life of 28 years, who fought many health issues of his own, be considered the most legendary person who has resided in a town since 1882?

It might take testimonies from some of the people who contributed their recollections of Thad Morgan in this book to present their argument. His life spanned two-thirds of the current "life" of Enterprise. His attending and serving the Enterprise public schools as a student, teacher, coach, assistant principal, principal, superintendent of schools, and consultant tallies up to more than 50 years.

BUT DON'T JUST THINK ABOUT THE NUMBERS. Think about the things that cannot be measured quantitatively. Think about the impact he has had and continues to have on the way our children are educated, how the quality of life is enjoyed by many of the people who reside in Enterprise, and the example he set for standing up for principles that all of us should believe in.

Think about those things, and THANK GOD FOR THAD MORGAN!

L-R Rick Rainer, Thad Morgan, Jim Reese, David Carter

"Passing the Torch"

Morgan – 1956 graduate of Enterprise High School. 37.5 years of service to the school system including 4 years as Assistant Principal at EHS; 5 years as Principal at EHS; and 22 years as Superintendent of Education. Retired June 30, 2001.

Reese – Succeeded Morgan as Superintendent in 2001. Graduate of EHS 1965. 37.5 years of service to school system. Oversaw the construction of 3 schools (2 caused by an EF4 tornado – see Rainer below). Retired December 31, 2010.

Carter – Succeeded Morgan as Principal of EHS 1979 and served 22 years in that position. 31 years of service to EHS including 5 years as Assistant Principal/Vocational Director from 1974-79. Retired June 30, 2001.

Rainer – Succeeded Carter as Principal of EHS. 23 years of service to school system including 12 years as Principal of EHS. Led EHS through turbulent times after the March 1, 2007 tornado that cost the lives of 8 students and destroyed the school. Students were displaced for 4 years. Retired June 30, 2012.

Printed in the USA
CPSIA information can be obtained
at www.ICGtesting.com
LVHW011051080124
768400LV00009B/386